THIRTY-FOUR STUDENTS

THIRTY-FOUR STUDENTS

A SCHOOL'S COLLECTION OF STORIES, POEMS, AND THOUGHTS

Limited Edition

By Greenway School

Greenway School Press

Thirty-four Students
A School's Collection of Stories,
Poems, and Thoughts

Cover design by Lynn Freeny
Interior Design by Ms. Alicia Harris
Edited by Lauren Swientoniewski,
Miranda Uphoff, and Jennifer Kitts
Software & PC advice by Nikki
Winters and Mr. Mark Young
Student photographs by Ken Kitts

For information:
Greenway School Press
A division of Greenway School
544 Canton Hollow Road
Knoxville, TN 37923
www.greenwayschool.edu

ISBN: 0-9714008-3-0

Printed in the United States of America

Dedication

This book is dedicated
to all middle schoolers
who think they cannot
make a difference
through their writing.

Preface

Middle schoolers are often the forgotten children of education. At Greenway School, we realize how very important the middle school years are. We have created a campus dedicated to the tween years of 11-14. In this community of learners, students are challenged to think for themselves, to question, to learn, and to grow. Writing, in every discipline, is a strong component of our program. In Language Arts, students often are given the freedom to write from their hearts and minds, to express their feelings and thoughts. The stories and poems in this book are the result of a Creative Writing Workshop in which the only criteria were to write every day and to edit and re-edit what was written. We proudly offer you ourselves…in writing.

Lynne Mullins

Acknowledgements

We would like to thank the following people.

Ms. Christine Duncan, founder of Greenway School
Lynn Freeny, book cover designer
Mr. Daryl Green, publishing expert
Ms. Alicia Harris, interior book designer
Ms. Lynne Mullins, Language Arts teacher
Lauren Swientoniewski, Miranda Uphoff, Jennifer Kitts, and Winton Burst, the publishing committee
Ms. Janet Torterelli, publishing assistant
Nikki Winters and Mr. Mark Young, computer software experts
Mr. Ken Kitts, photographer

Animal Stories

Jennifer Kitts
Chelsea Oliver

Bingo Burns

Jennifer Kitts

Hello, my name is Bingo Burns. First of all, I am a dog with an IQ of the above average adult. I got my first name from my ex-owner, Mildred, who did not understand my superiority. So she yelled "bingo" because she thought she'd won something, but what she didn't know was that I was selling her on eBay! I had just checked in and the bidding had reached $2,000,000 but I had shown a picture of her from when she was in high school. She's 84 now. She has so many wrinkles that you can't see her eyes and she wears her hair in pigtails just like in the "good old days." Oh, did I forget to mention that her hair is white on one side and black on the other? She gets her fashion tips from Disney movies. She is also very fat and fails to realize that mini skirts don't work for people who are 400 lb. I, on the other hand, get my fashion tips from Abercrombie and Fetch. I'm personally into plaid and squether, "squirrel leather."

Back to her yelling at me. "Doggie! Get off the expensive furniture! You little dog! You get to spend the night in the doghouse and I know you'll love that," said Mildred wildly.

"Oh, shut up! You're speaking to a dog with an IQ of an above average adult!" Bingo yelled.

Unfortunately for Bingo, Mildred never heard him because Mildred can't hear unless you're speaking loudly.

Oh, by the way, the doghouse they're talking about is one that has a white picket fence just big enough so a Scotty dog could not get through. The doghouse is Victorian styled, four "dog stories " high, and one human story. The doghouse has a ramp and a porch that goes around the front of the house. Bingo personally installed four flat-screen TV's, that he uses for adding to his intellectual mind. But this has nothing to do with the task at hand.

Bingo hates the doghouse unless he is in a good mood, which happens very rarely. Back to the fight…

Bingo yelled at Mildred loudly, "You dog!"

"BINGO," yelled Mildred.

"I'm going to the doghouse to think things over without you wailing about how I'm ruining your expensive assets," Bingo announced. Of course he wasn't going to think things over. He was going to focus on his relationship with his girlfriend, Amy, who is a Yorkshire terrier.

I've caught two squirrels for my girlfriend Amy just this week. Oh! Here she comes. I can see her glamorous brown eyes, her golden brown and radiant black hair tied up in two pigtails with pink hair bows, her squirrel tail scarf with the carved bone pin made by yours truly, and her Abercrombie and Fetch pink plaid dog coat. She's almost too glamorous for words!

What, can it be true? She's… she's talking to Bob!!!!!!! He's a wimpy wiener dog and he's talking to my Yorkie, my Amy! My Amy with the golden brown and radiant black hair twinkling, and her glistening brown eyes that look so beautiful. Oh why bother? They're only friends, but I use to only be friends with Amy too! Maybe Bob wants to be more than friends! He's going down!!!

In half a second Bingo had bitten poor Bob's ear when at that second…

Amy spoke or rather barked, "What are you doing!"

"Oh I was wondering what you guys were talking about," Bingo asked calmly.

"You could have just asked us!" Bob said nervously. "You didn't have to bite my ear!"

"If you really must know he was just trying to get a date with Claire, my friend, the tea cup poodle," Amy said impatiently.

"Yeah, I *was* trying to get a date, but now my ear is all messed up so now I'll never get one," Bob said with great caution.

"Oh, come on Bob, she likes a fighter, so you'll be fine. But as for you, Bingo, I'll deal with you later," Amy snarled.

"O.K., see you then," Bingo said happily.

Then I watched Amy and that other dog walk down the street. My heart filled with love and hatred although I could not figure out which of them I loved or hated. So I went home and tried to sleep.

It was a dark and dreary night and only one soul was awake …It was Bingo Burns typing away on IM's. The beginning of every conversation was "Hello! The first thing you should know is I am a dog with the IQ of an above average adult. My name… is…Bingo Burns!

The only sad thing was that was the end of the conversation too. But life is life and you deal with it. So Bingo decided to go downstairs and see what was edible on the table: potato chips, pizza, apple pie, or maybe even flan!

Broccoli! Bingo howled into nothingness.

Broccoli. That's all? That's the only thing on the table. Bingo howled into nothingness again, but this time Mildred had heard him.

This is never good for a food thief. Ever.

"BINGO! Is that you?" Mildred snarled.

Bingo laughed to himself. Remember Mildred can't hear well. Bingo was going to take that and run with it. Literately run with it! Bingo jumped up on the hand polished marble, skidding a little, and grabbed the broccoli, sending to the floor the crystal plate that only a second ago had had broccoli on it.

"Bingo now I know that's you," Mildred yelled down the stairs from her extra bed that was completely black. "You don't want me to come down there do you?" Mildred yawned.

Of course Bingo was long gone from there. In fact he was back in his doghouse, logged onto eBay to see how high the bids for Mildred had gotten. Somehow the site was messed up.The bid was 3 cents. How could that be? Then he looked at the picture and he was appalled. Mildred had found the ad, put a very recent picture in and erased the bids. "Why would she do this?" Bingo asked himself.

Bingo decided to call it a night. So he wriggled out of his

Abercrobie and Fetch clothes and into his custom-made silk nightshirt and went to bed.

At about twelve noon Bingo got up and called Amy's doghouse phone. No answer. So Bingo had to go to extremes. He had to call Claire, the tea cup poodle, and trust me, he didn't want to. Bingo, extremely reluctant as he was, painstakingly dialed the numbers into his cell phone.

A preppy voice came on the phone. "HELLO, this is Claire. Do you want to compliment me on my good looks or do you just want to talk about me. I kno…"

"I just want to talk to Amy if she's there," Bingo said flatly.

"Oh," Claire said sharply, "here she is and don't take long. You're going to waste my minutes!"

"Claire who is this?" Amy asked. (Bingo could hear that the phone was held out.) "Oh, it's your stupid boy friend," Claire said with a glare.

"He's not stupid," Amy said.

"HELLO, I'M STILL ON THE PHONE!" Bingo yelled.

"Oh hello," Amy said.

"Uh, hi Amy. To get straight to the point, I was wondering if you would like to go out tonight? There's a new Italian restaurant that's pretty good. They serve huge portions so there has got to be all sorts of stuff in the dumpster," Bingo said happily.

"I'd love to," Amy exclaimed.

"Okay see you there," Bingo said.

Click the phones turned off.

Bingo then went into his collar closet and picked out an elegant brown leather collar. Then he went into his clothes closet and came out wearing a leather jacket and an Abercrombie and Fetch shirt with a tennis ball on it. Bingo combed his hair and polished his toenails to get rid of any dirt.

"I'm done," Bingo said with a sigh.

Bingo walked out of his doghouse straight into Mildred.

"Bingo," Mildred said in an odd way, "I've been waiting for you!" Mildred picked Bingo up and shoved him into a doggie bag.

Bingo said in a happy voice, "So you had a bad game of croquet?"

"Now no one can hear you scream," Mildred said in an evil voice. "I will never hear you insult me again. You will never use the computer again. You will never break my fine china again. You will never put your dirty feet on my couch again. Now I am going to tell you what I'm going to do to you. I'm going to send you to Timbuctu. That's right, Bingo, I'm going to send you so far away you'll never make it back alive."

You may think Bingo has lost all hope and will now condemn himself, but remember Bingo is very smart. He does have an IQ of an above average adult. What Mildred doesn't know is that Bingo is familiar with the mail service and he knows about return addresses and that if you don't put on the return address, the post office will return the package. However, Bingo decided to chew his way out because he wasn't going to depend on Mildred to mess up. She always tends to do things right when you need her to mess up.

As soon as Mildred had left the package with Bingo crammed

inside, Bingo opened his jaws and bit the doggie bag thinking of Mildred. In two bites he was free. Bingo then ran to the nearest pay phone.

"Hello, police. This is Bingo. I was almost killed by my owner. She's my mom, but she makes me call her owner. She lives in Bay View, California. Will you arrest her? She tried to kill me," Bingo said sadly.

"We'll be right over," the policeman said in a strong, but shaky voice.

"Thank you so much sir," Bingo said in a fake scared voice.

Bingo snuck back home and dipped his feet in mud and ran up and down the couch. Then he "accidentally" tipped over the fine china cabinet. Then he went to evil owners.com where he got some revenge tips for Mildred. Then Bingo called Mildred an old bag. Mildred heard and ran downstairs and picked Bingo up.

"I'm gonna kill you dog!" she yelled wildly.

Mildred turned the blender on high and picked up Bingo. Mildred lowered Bingo just enough so that some of the hair on his head got chopped off.

"Put the dog down and no one gets hurt!" a police officer said. "You are now under arrest for animal abuse!" another policeman said in a loud intimidating voice.

"Okay," Mildred said in a small voice, "how did you get here?" Mildred put Bingo down on the ground.

"We got a call from your son," the police officer said as he picked up Bingo and petted him.

"I don't have a son," Mildred said.

The police officer answered, "We know. We checked your records and found that you had an interesting dog. So we came over to take the dog to a nice home, but then we saw that in your will you leave the house and all belongings to your dog."

Bingo said, with impatience "My name is Bingo. Can I leave? I'm late for a date with…"

"You can't leave until we settle this," the police said.

"Ma'am put your hands behind your back," the police said.

"We deal with people like you all the time."

Then they carried Mildred out on a stretcher with wheels on account of the fact that she's 400 lbs. Six months later, a jury put Mildred in prison for thirty years. Remember Mildred is 84. The jury also gave the deeds to the house to Bingo who now has a Mohawk due to the blender incident. He took all of Mildred's clothes and jewelry and founded a NO KILL animal shelter for dogs.

Bingo married Amy. They had six children and adopted one who they named Bingo Philip Burns. He was a pure bred Scottie dog. Bingo, Amy, Kel, Spot, Lila, Macy, Kenneth, Luck, and Bingo Philip Burns all lived as close to happily ever after as any real person, or animal, ever did.

Afterlife

Chelsea Oliver

As the car rolled over I saw my life flash before me. Would I ever see my family again? Suddenly I woke up and I was being licked by a dog. A dog ! Where was I? Was this an afterlife? Suddenly all those questions became clear. I was a newborn puppy. This *was* the afterlife. But this wasn't right. I was in the same house with the same people. Then I remembered our dog Lucy was expecting puppies. Somebody picked me up and put something around my neck. Then they set me down next all the other puppies. I fell asleep.

I woke when my human sister picked me up. She was talking about how cute I was and if she could keep me. Then suddenly she put this thing that looked like a shot in my mouth only it wasn't a shot; Yuck, this liquid went into my mouth. I was being wormed and it tasted awful! Then my human mother-owner told my human sister to put me back against Lucy and let me sleep. I went over and lay down. All the other puppies toppled on me so I was on the bottom.

I woke up and I was hungry! I ate and I went over to the other puppies. I started to play with them. We played games. Then my human sister picked me up and said, "Hello." She dressed me in this really ugly dress and started playing tea party with me. She put me in a carriage and rolled it around like I was a baby doll. Finally she took off the dress and set me down with the other puppies.

It was a couple of weeks later when they let us out into the yard for the first time. It was so good to have the sunshine on my body again and to feel the grass on my feet. I rolled around some and chewed on some sticks in the yard. They took off the string on my neck and put a collar on and connected a leash to it. We went outside and took a walk. The wind felt good against my fur. A paperboy passed by on a bike. All sorts of cars passed by and some had their radios on. We walked on for awhile and then we turned around and went back.

The next day they took my dog mom away and put a bowl of dog food for each of us on the floor. When I was hungry, I went over and tasted it. It wasn't that bad. I ate the rest of it and went and played with the others. They gave us doggie toys. I chewed on one and played tug -o-war with another. The toys were all a lot of fun.

It was one particular day when I first saw the mailman. He was wearing a really tacky blue and white uniform. He had a bottle that looked like tear gas. I didn't like him because he looked really mean. I barked at him. Finally, he walked away.

Today was my first time going to the vet. It was also my first time in a car. My human family put a carrier in the back of the car. I sat in my human sister's lap. The radio was playing cool music. The window was open so I stuck my head out and it was windy! There were cars outside. I barked at them as they passed by. Finally we got to the vet place. My human sister put me in the carrier with the other puppies and took us inside. I was a little scared. A strange lady picked me up and weighed me. She looked inside my mouth and nose. She also looked at my eyes and at the underside of my paws. She gave me a shot and it was all over. I went home. I wouldn't have been so scared if all the other animals hadn't left all of those scary smells.

One day I was playing with the other puppies when my human sister picked me up. She put this stuff on my back. It was gross! It was wet and sticky. I tried to shake it off, but it wouldn't come off. Finally I gave up and went to play again. I wonder what that icky stuff was?

Today I experienced my first bath. It was fun! My human sister picked me up and put me in the tub. She put some shampoo on me and scrubbed me all over. There was this interesting white bar sitting next to me. It looked like it would taste good. I started to eat it, but my human sister said "No don't do that." So I had to stop. My human sister picked me up and dried me with some fluffy towels. She put me back with the other puppies.

It was some months later when everyone started to get ready for Christmas. They hung up lights and decorations. They got a big tree and put it in the living room. I chewed on one of the branches, but I didn't do that again because my human family said not to do it. They hung lights and ornaments on the tree. They hung stockings on the mantelpiece. It was the night before Christmas. They put cookies and milk on the mantelpiece. They went to bed, but before my human mom and dad went to bed, they put presents under the tree and they filled the stockings. They also put bows around all of the puppies and left us in the living room and they left a note too. In the morning, my human sister opened her presents and she also unpacked her stocking. Finally, she read the note and smiled because the note said she could keep all of us. We all lived happily in our house.

Fairy Tales Old and New

Hannah Cunningham
Sarah LeMense
Lauren Swientoniewski
Kelsey Worsham

Princess Cilicia

Hannah Cunningham

Forget everything anyone has ever told you about fairy tales. The prince doesn't always do the rescuing and the princess isn't always the one in distress. In this particular fairy tale, the prince is the one in trouble and it's the princess's job to do the rescuing.

Now let's meet the characters. Cilicia is the princess and Charming is the prince. As usual there is an evil witch and a fairy godmother.

One day the prince, Charming, who was indeed quite

repulsive, was walking down a path in the woods when he met Amora, who is the evil witch. She asked him what he was doing there.

"I am taking a walk in the woods. What does it look like I'm doing, fighting a dragon or something?"

Amora took quite a bit of offense at his last comment, seeing as she ***was*** blind and all. "I will put a curse on you for being one of the most rude young princes I've ever met. Unless you would rather be locked up in a tower."

Charming replied, "If I am the most rude prince you've ever met, rudest prince would be better. How many princes do you know?"

Now Amora was really mad. Even though she had given Charming a choice between a curse or the tower, she knew, now, that both had to be done.

Since his name was Charming and he was so absolutely revolting, Amora made him the most handsome man ever to live, in her opinion. Now, instead of being short, weak and kind of fat, he was tall and muscular. His greasy red hair was replaced by beautiful, dark brown waves. Unfortunately, only part of the curse had worked because Charming was still as rude and impolite as ever. The idea had been to make him the most perfect and charming man alive, show him off at Queen Arialla's ball, hoping he and the beautiful Princess Cilicia would fall in love. After the ball, Amora would lock him up in the Tower, hoping that the princess would come to save him and she too would die.

Meanwhile, on the other side of the Kingdom, in the bottom floor of the shortest tower sat the beautiful princess, Cilicia, in this story, me. Yes, that's right. ***I*** am the most beautiful, and only, princess in the surrounding area.

I am ***so*** looking forward to the ball tomorrow. I have heard that every prince, and any other man with a good and rich family, in the area will be there. This should be a very good chance for me, or should I say my parents, to choose my husband.

Now back to Prince Charming…

Amora had taken him back to her house, not a witch's house like the one in Hansel and Gretel. Oh no, most definitely not. This house had to be the sole scariest and most evil place on the face of the Earth, or any planet for that matter.

Amora had tied Charming to a chair. She didn't use rope or any kind of tape. She had this spell that is equal to duct tape, but without the tape.

Anyway, Amora couldn't figure out what had gone wrong. Charming was still so mean-spirited, she thought. Maybe if I could let him meet the Princess, her goodness would rub off on him. Boy was she wrong.

It turns out, the perfect princess image is just that, an image. I'm not the perfect young lady I'm cracked up to be. As a matter of fact I can be downright mean. I mean, I can be a lady and all, when I try, but if you catch me on the wrong day, oh boy are you in for it.

Anyway, tomorrow is the ball that is meant to celebrate the fact that my parents think I'm of the age to marry. Of course in matters like this, my opinion doesn't matter. I don't think I ever want to get married, at least not to any of their choices. The only input I've had in this ball is picking out my dress, the lesser of the horrid dresses my parents picked out.

Being a princess sometimes can be awful, but other times it can be great. Having people wait on you hand on foot really isn't that bad, and some of my brother's servants, well… let's just say, if they were princes I might not have such a hard time finding a husband.

The ball will be dreadful. I have been to other balls that my parents have thrown. Those were some of the most boring nights of my life with all these people dancing and being all proper. It really was awful. You should have seen it.

And this one isn't going to be any better. The whole reason for this ball is for me to meet all potential husbands so my parents can make their choice. The one thing that might make this ball okay--compared to the rest-- is, ***it's all about me***! I'm going to get all the attention and, even though I don't have any say in anything, it looks like the ball is my idea and I get all the credit.

Now to the guy I will marry. Of course I don't know it until after the ball, but anyway we're going to get married.

His name is Tom. And he is Prince Charming's man in waiting. Yes, that is his title. It does sound very strange, but remember, he works for the prince, Charming.

Besides working for him, Tom is Charming's brother. Neither of them knows it, yet, and no one would ever be able to tell. They are polar opposites. Tom is everything Charming isn't. Tom is charming, handsome and the nicest person any one could ever want to meet. He is so kind and selfless. I know. Nobody's perfect, but he is pretty darn close.

The beautiful princess Cilicia, wait that's me, I am getting so excited telling this story that I forgot I am the Narrator. Anyway, I save Tom, the real Prince Charming and save Charming after he falls out the window into thorns when I say I wouldn't marry him.

Amora gets what she deserves. I know what you're thinking. " Oh the bad witch, she gets water poured on her and melts." Well, you're wrong. She gets her sight back. And now she helps the optometrists, eye doctors, cure blindness in children, no less.

Like most fairy tales, everyone who deserves to, lives happily ever after.

The Sailor

Sarah LeMense

A girl name Camry and her father were sailing off to sea on another long journey of her father's. Camry didn't have a mother, or so she thought, and her father was a blacksmith whose passion was to sail. As the waves licked the side of the boat, Camry asked her father to tell her a story. As usual, he told her about the ocean and the creatures that live in its depth. He told her about creatures she only dreamed about and shortly she was dreaming because her father usually did that to her with his stories.

Her father continued on his way, praying that it was going to be a wonderful journey. Not like the one eight years ago…

Camry awoke to the smell of salt water and fish. She was use to the smell and had a gurgling feeling in her stomach. Her father was fishing for their supper. Camry was still tired and she was starting to get a little cold. So, she snuggled up to her father and watched the dolphins playing a few feet from them. She didn't like her father fishing so close to them, but at the same time, she was starved, so let him continue on.

When morning came, they were already half way back to the shore. Camry had a feeling that she heard her name being called over and over again. It wasn't her father's voice, and it sounded like a woman. It was distant and lonely sounding. Her father didn't seem to notice the sound, and Camry was very confused.

When they got back to shore, they went on with their daily life. Camry though she would just keep the secret of the voice to herself.

When the time came for her to go sailing again, Camry was ready and very interested in everything.

When she got on the boat, she went straight to her favorite spot and opened her ears.

It was a long time before she heard her name again. It appeared her father had heard it too because he turned around. The sound was getting louder as her father came closer to her. Camry saw her father's eyes drift to the waves, get big, and quickly shift back to her. Camry turned her head, but was then quickly stopped by her father.

He said, "Camry, there is something I have to tell you." She had never heard that sound in her father's voice and was quickly worried.

Her father began, "Eight years ago, when you were only a babe, I took you and your mother for a boat ride. Everything was wonderful and the winds were perfect. The only thing I didn't know was that your mother was going to transform."

He quickly glanced to the spot where he had looked before and started to speak again. "See your mother is a mermaid and had had a curse laid upon her to be human for twenty years. She had told me about this, but I thought she was only joking. She also didn't tell me that any child she birthed would become a mermaid or merman. You are now the age where you should become a mermaid. I had forgotten about this. Now, your mother is calling, asking you to come join her. It is your choice. My decision would be to go with her to explore the ocean."

Camry saw the hurt in her father's eyes even though he tried to cover it up. She knew he wanted her to stay with him.

Camry knew what she had to do. She wanted to go with her mother, but first she must talk to her. She told her father this and he agreed. He called her over and immediately hugged her. She got this warm feeling inside. She knew she would go with her mother. She got up, packed her favorite treasures, and gave her father a long hug goodbye. He grabbed her and tucked her in his arms, whispering in her ear to stay safe. He kissed her goodbye, and she jumped into the ocean.

As soon as she was in the water, her feet turned to fins and she could breathe underwater. Her mother swam over, cradled her, and stroked her hair. It had been eight years since she had seen her little girl and she wouldn't let her go. Camry felt shy and loved at the same time. Her mother showed her the ocean and whispered things in her ear.

Camry had lived in the ocean for four years when she saw the familiar sailboat in the water. Her mother had told her never to go above the waters, but she just had to do it. She saw her father's hair as he was looking down. She wanted to see what he was looking at, so she circled the boat cautiously. When she peered into the boat, she saw her father was looking at a picture of her. He looked sick and very alone.

Camry started to cry and swam to her mother. Her mother was very welcoming. Camry told her what had happened. Her mother sighed loudly and Camry knew what she had to do. She packed her things and tried to kiss her mother goodbye, but her mother would not let go. She said, "Come with me my child. I want to come with you."

Camry followed her mother into a cave. A small fish was sitting there. Camry heard a weird language and all of a sudden the fish circled her mother and her so fast that Camry fell over. When the circling stopped, she and her mother were human.

They swam quickly to the surface. Her father's boat was about five feet a way. Camry cried out to her father. He turned around and saw his daughter and his wife.

He sailed over to them, picked Camry up, and pulled her mother out of the water. As soon as they were out of the water, their fins turned to feet. Camry hugged her father and looked at him. He had this wonderful smile, a smile she had seen once before. The smile that was in his wedding picture that she had seen in her mother's home in the ocean. It was a wonderful feeling to have her family back together at last and everyone was happy.

As Camry listened to her father telling her the things that had happened while she was gone, she snuggled up to her mother and fell asleep as they sailed into the sunset.

My Happily Ever After

Lauren Swientoniewski

Some people would call me lucky. Some would tell me I am spoiled. Some people say that I should have not been born. Some people would not even know who I was until they saw me, and by that time they would have regretted it.

Many stories about a beautiful girl born to the King and Queen start with "Once upon a time," but mine doesn't. In a huge town, the King and Queen had three ugly daughters. They were so ugly that the King and Queen would not even let them out of the castle because they were scared that the nearby kingdom would declare war. But I was different.

When I was born, everyone in the castle had their eyes closed in fear that my ugliness would burn their eyes. So when I was born, it was quiet in the room. Some of the maids opened their eyes and breathed a sigh of relief. When my mother heard that everything was all right and nobody died, she opened her eyes and looked at her new baby.

When she looked at me, I could see the happiness in her eyes. I could also see vanity. I had golden hair and skin that when you touched it, you would have thought you were back in your crib it was so soft! My eyes were as soft and as blue as the sky. I was completely the opposite of my siblings. My mother ordered everyone out of the room. She was stroking my head and telling herself, "She's mine. All mine! I will make sure that the most prettiest princess of the world will not be spoiled by someone else!" Then she ordered my maidservant to take me to the tower and be locked away from the rest of the world.

When I was taken away from my mother, I was placed very carefully in a huge cradle that was very soft. Around me were many stuffed animals that seemed to always be watching me. But I never cried and I never spoke the words a baby speaks. I was just there.

I know many of these things about me when I was a baby because my maidservant, Mary, was always in and out of my huge castle tower. The day after I was born, I heard my mother, the Queen, talking to Mary. Mary said, "You need to name this child, Your Highness. If she is going to be a fancy to all princes, then she needs to have a proper title."

" Mary, you just be quiet! I am the mother of this girl and you do not have the right to boss me around!" the Queen replied stubbornly.

" Well I guess you're right!" Mary replied matter-of-factly.

"Of course I'm right."

"Oh well, but back to the child..."

"If you say one more thing about her, your head will be off your body in no time at all!"

"Fine!"

"So I have found a perfect name for her. Her name shall be Diamond and that is that!"

And with a swish of the Queen's dress, she went down the tower stairs. There was a soft knock at my door. Mary stepped in. She then came over to my crib and looked at me. Her face was so sad that I could feel tears welling up in my eyes. I began to cry. I yelled and screamed at the top of my lungs. I heard footsteps outside my door. I knew it was my mother. She barged in and started yelling at Mary. I began to cry louder. Finally when the bickering stopped, I stopped. Then the Queen yelled, " You're a witch! I knew it all along!"

" Yes, I know I am a witch! And I am going to put a little spell on this daughter of yours so that neither you nor she will be happy for the rest of your lives!"

With a flick of her hand she said " Diamond will take no fancy to any prince she meets!" Then she was gone.

This spell was the most horrible thing that had ever happened to my mother. First she already had three extremely ugly daughters, and to go along with that, her prettiest daughter will never marry a rich prince. For the next week, her whole schedule only had crying and complaining about her life. But I did not care at the moment.

It has been fifteen years ago since that day in the tower. I was, of course, moved to a new tower. Ever since I was not allowed to leave my room. After all the years of mourning, my mother almost completely forgot about me. She probably thought that if I was not going to be married to a royal man, then I was not worth thinking about. The only thing that I suffered from the spell is that I am never allowed to leave my room. Every morning I look out my window and see a young man, about the same age as me, walk through the woods nearby the castle. My dream was that one-day I would be able to meet him.

It sounds like my life was horrible, but it was okay. My room was nothing that you would believe. The ceilings were high and seemed to go on forever since it was a tower. My walls were purple. Not a purple that was so bright it burns, but the purple that was soft, like a lilac. Different kinds of flowers were painted on the wall and there were millions of scattered diamonds on the wall. I also had gold molding that glittered when the sun came though the window. I loved it, but what I wanted more was freedom.

Every day seemed to drag on forever. Every day was the same and every day I would be mocked and teased by my three sisters. Since they were the age of marriage, very often a prince of a far away kingdom would come and visit. My mother now would try to get me interested in all the stuck up, self centered, and daft princes, but I didn't like any of them.

As I said, the princes were daft, and each one of my ugly sisters was married off and finally I was the only sibling left in the castle. By each day, my mother had given up on me. I just did not fall in love with anyone. Except the young boy in the woods every morning.

I finally decided that I would run away and become a town's person. Maybe then I would have more freedom to do anything I want. So I planned my escape.

The next morning I got up bright and early. I quietly crept down to the kitchen and took a small muffin and ate it for breakfast. Then I went back to my tower room and rummaged through my closet. There were many beautiful dresses, the kind princesses wear, but I was no longer a princess. I searched until I found a plain dress with a cloak and some matching shoes. The dress came to my ankles and was a pale lilac and the shoes were a dark purple. It wasn't like a town's person, but it would have to do.

Quickly and quietly I ran down the huge corridor stairs. My feet made a small tapping sound on the stone. I could feel through my shoe the coldness. "Winter is almost here." I thought to myself. When I reached the bottom of the staircase, I could hear the sound of the morning. I needed to be quick. I ran towards the escape door. It was a small door that only the royal family knew of. When I reached for the lock, I could feel a presence behind me. Then I could feel a cold hand on my shoulder.

I wanted to scream, but a hand over my mouth would not let me. “Be quiet, Diamond. I don’t want anyone to hear you!” a voice behind me said.

I turned around and was amazed that it was my father who was speaking. I could barely remember him because he was always on these “quests”. I replied “What are you doing here?”

“ I should be asking the same.”

“ I don’t like my life stuck up in a tower so I am running away. But please don’t tell mother!”

“ Of course, but it is not safe out there…”

“ Safe? You are telling me to be safe? All these years you had been on these ‘quests’, forgetting about me! And you are telling me to be safe! I am not listening to you!"

So I tied the cloak around my neck and I opened the door. As I was climbing down the passageway, I could hear a quiet sobbing. Then I heard my father say, " Don't worry, Diamond. I will always be with you and I will always keep an eye on you. Just don't worry!" And then I slipped and started to fall into the darkness.

The tunnel ended by a small creek near the edge of the town. I could hear the sound of the town: the horses' hooves on the cobblestone, shouts, and many other various things. I couldn't go back. So I walked toward the village.

I thought that I would fit in, but I was wrong. There were people who I thought could not live another day. On the corner of the street, there was a young lady with two children begging for money. I took out two small coins from my pocket and placed one in each of the children's hands. When they looked up, I could see a slight smile in their eyes. The mother looked at me and smiled. "Thank you," she said. I nodded and walked off.

Soon after I ran into a problem. All the girls' hair were dirty, but mine was a golden blonde that felt like silk. I needed to do something. Down the street was a hair shop. So I ran inside.

Inside was an old man and he was working on a young man. "I'll be with you in a moment. Just sit down in those chairs over there." I sat down. I was not trying, but I was listening to their conversation. "So what is the latest gossip in the village today?" the old man said.

"You mean you haven't heard? Princess Diamond has escaped mysteriously and they don't even know how she got out of the castle. It is heavily guarded."

"But half of the time the guards do not know what was going on! They are almost as dumb as cows!"

"True, but the Queen is furious. She will do anything to get that child back."

"Yes, but…"

They both turned around and looked at me. They were looking at me like I had something wrong with me. "Look!" the young man said,

"That is the princess! I know it because of her diamond necklace!"

I know I have not told you about my necklace. Each of my sisters had a necklace with a certain jewel. Since my name is "Diamond", I had a diamond necklace. The men started toward me. I ran out into the street and started running.

As I was running, I could hear the two men behind me. I ran down main roads and alleyways. I knew it was a risk because I heard many times how people would go into the alleys and never be seen again. I shivered. I turned into a tight alley and sped up. I thought that it would never end. But then I felt another cold hand on my shoulder. I was pulled into a gap in the wall of a building. I stifled a scream, but a hand was placed over my mouth.

It was dark so I could not see who it was. But he said "Quiet. Those men want to kill you like you're some runaway princess or something. You can come with me to my cottage and I'll keep you away from those kinds of people." I wanted to tell him I was a princess, but I went against it.

We ran quickly down the dark alleyway and finally we were out. He led me into the woods beside the village. Then we stopped in a small clearing and I immediately recognized the area. It was the clearing beside my tower. This was the clearing where, every morning, I would see the young man. I then turned around and my rescuer was that young man.

I saw that he was looking at my neck. I remembered that I still had my true identity on, which was my diamond necklace. I then tore the necklace off and threw it down to the ground. I was sad that I had to get rid of something so valuable and pretty, but I just had to do it.

After that I looked up to the man. It was the young man who walked though the woods every morning. I couldn't believe it. He motioned with his hand to follow him, so I did.

I really wanted to start a conversation with him while we were walking through the woods to his home. So I said, "Thank you for saving me."

"No problem." he replied.

"Would you mind to tell me your name?" There was a short pause. Then he said, "Devin is my name. And yours?"

This was a problem. I could not tell him my real name. "Claire." So far, so good… It appeared that he had not found out yet. We walked further. Then, in the distance, I could see a small cottage. There was smoke coming out of the chimney. Finally we reached the door. Before he went inside, he turned to me. "This is my house. I live alone but there is an extra bedroom in the back. I'll give you food and anything else you need," Devin briskly told her. He went inside. "Wait!" I shouted, "What do you do for a living?"

"I chop wood," Devin said, sounding ashamed.

"Well, it is not that bad, compared to what I had to do," I said, and I went inside.

I have been living with Devin for two months now. We have become great friends and sometimes I would help him with the firewood. Usually I would take care of household chores. Slowly my hair and skin became darker and I looked more and more like a normal person. And all this time he has not found out about my true self.

I am not one of those people who are for lying, but at certain times it is necessary. Yes, I did have to make many things up about myself. It was awkward at first, but I got used to it.

Everything was fine until one day, and that was the day I thought my life was ruined. It all started when I went into the woods to gather water for the bath. As I was filling up the bowl, I heard a rustle behind me. I turned around and there was…my father.

"What are you doing here?" I said to him.

"Well, Diamond, I know that you are in love with Devin, but I want you to know…" my father replied.

"I don't want your opinion," I interrupted.

"Well, he is the prince of..."

My father did not have to say any more. Almost immediately after I knew he was a prince, I could feel the effect of the spell. I had no love for Devin anymore. I started to cry. I had always thought that the spell had done me a great thing, but now since I had finally found a prince who was good enough, all was lost. I just had to find a way to break the spell.

I turned back to my father. "How can I break the spell?" I cried to him.

"That I do not know, but I do know where you can talk to the witch who caused this all. She lives in the deepest part of the woods. That is all I know." He said solemnly.

So I stood up and started deeper into the woods. I didn't even say good bye to my father.

I couldn't give up. My legs and my whole body ached because of walking. Finally I declared that I was lost. When I almost turned around to try to find my way back, the trees opened up to a clearing. In the center was a large cottage. “This must be the place,” I thought to myself. So I approached the front door and knocked.

“Who’s there?” an old and scratchy voice said from the inside of the house.

“Diamond, Diamond.”

“Oh yes, an old acquaintance. Come on in.”

The door opened slowly and I peered inside. Inside there were thousands of different bottles filled with brightly colored potions. It scared me half to death. When I entered, I could see Mary, the witch who was my maidservant when I was a baby. She was older now, with wrinkles and a cane. She stood up. “Now what is wrong today?” she asked me with a dirty smile.

I told her that I wanted the spell to be broken. Afterward she was blabbing on about how it is hard to do that and she might not be able to do it. Then a flicker of evil went though her eyes and she said, “I will not do it, unless I have your diamond necklace. Give it to my tomorrow at noon, or I will never break the spell.”

I ran out of the house crying. I ran through the woods until I reached a small pool at the bottom of a waterfall. I fell onto my knees and wept. No way could I ever get that necklace in time. First, I was lost in the woods and I did not know where the clearing was and second probably someone had already picked up the necklace. I was ruined.

I stopped crying and I just sat by the water. I had no clue where I was. At least I could try to find my way back to Devin's house. I stood up and started walking on the direction that I thought was the way home. Maybe I should just go back to the castle and live a life alone. "No," I said under my breath, "I have a life too and I can not let people run over me like this!" So I ran.

It was a miracle that I could find my way to Devin's house. He was outside waiting for me. Beside him was my father. Oh great. He probably caused more trouble. I came up to them. Devin was frowning. "Why did you lie to me?" he thundered at me.

"I didn't know if you would like me being a princess, but now that I know that you are a prince…"

"It doesn't matter now. Just take this. Your father gave it to me."

Devin placed my diamond necklace into my hands. It felt so great to have it back again. I guess that Devin knew about the spell from my father and that I needed to break the spell with the necklace. I didn't care where he found it. I just ran into the woods and I kept running until I found the cottage. I did not care if I got lost. Finally I reached the cottage and burst opened the door.

"I got it, Mary! You can break the spell now that I have the diamond necklace!" I yelled. I could see the witch's madness. I threw it at her feet and she picked it up. She clenched it in her fist. She thought I wouldn't get it.

"Fine," she said. She went over to her shelves filled with bottles and took out one that had a thick pink powder in it. She took a pinch out and sprinkled it over my head. My whole body tingled with excitement. I was hovering over the ground. There was a glow coming from my skin. I was placed gently on the ground. When I was back on my feet, I ran out of the house and I saw Devin waiting for me. I loved him again. He then gave me something in a box. I opened it and saw another diamond necklace.

Well, if you didn't guess, Devin and I were married almost immediately. At the wedding, my mother and father were there. After the whole time I was gone, she became less vain and accepted my darker hair and skin. Even my sisters came. All of us had a great time. After the wedding, I moved in with Devin in his cottage. So in the end, I guess that I had a happily ever after.

Cinderella at the Bar Mitzvah

Kelsey Worsham

"Wake up!" Gloria yelled.

Hal opened her eyes and wondered where she was. She remembered running towards the kitchen, worried because her father was not home yet. Her step-mom, Gloria, and her two spoiled brats were crowded around her blue bedroom. Susie and Mallory, the two spoiled brats, were perched upon a large blue beanbag. Gloria was giving 'the eye' to Mouse. Mouse is a large golden retriever who enjoys chewing on tennis balls.

"Hal is fine, mommy! Can we go?" Mallory whined.

"Yeah. What she said!" Susie pitched in.

Gloria turned her back on Hal and walked out of the room with her two favorite children.

"Well, Mouse. What happened?" Hal said to her dog.

Mouse walked out of the room, soon barking at something down the hall. Probably the Evil step-relatives… Hal was alarmed when her bright green phone began ringing. She held it to her ear and made herself sound extra-ill.

"Hey, Haley. What's up? Are you okay? Robby's been saying that you were pretty sick or something," Hal's best friend, Dalia, said.

"Oh, Dalia! I just don't know what happened. But the step twins seemed to care so much. NOT. How is Robby?" Hal murmured.

"Robby is fine. Isn't it cool we're still best friends? I mean, since 3rd grade we've been inseparable." Dalia yelled from the other line.

"Yeah. Hey, I have to go. Mallory's walking in," Hal whispered.

Mallory took a seat on Hal's bed and smoothed down her new

skirt that she was wearing. Then, Mallory looked about the room and smirked.

"Ha. You're room just has a bed! Mine has a TV, a dresser, and even a pink…" Mallory began to say.

"That's great, Mallory. Now why don't you stop gloating and go find Glenda and Harry?" Hal said quietly. Glenda and Harry were Mallory's best friends.

Mallory glared at Hal and walked towards the door. Then, she looked pleased.

"Speaking of Harry, his brother is having his Bar Mitzvah. His name is Gerry, isn't it?" Mallory said, looking innocently towards Hal.

"Stop it, Mallory! Just because Gerry is 'popular' and likes me better than you doesn't mean you have to rub it in! It isn't my fault your mom hates me and she grounded me exactly on the day of his Bar Mitzvah!" Hal yelled. She slammed the door in Mallory's face.

The next morning, Hal took her usual route to school. It just wasn't the same since her dad had died. It turned out that while she was waiting for him at the apartment, he had been in a car wreck. It was awful. When Hal found out, she hyperventilated. The local news came and Gloria said nice things to Hal in front of the camera. Gloria's life is a big bluff. As Hal walked past Dalia's house, she looked at the front gate. Dalia was walking towards the gate, dressed in a multi-colored, over sized, poncho.

"Isn't my outfit *tres* beautiful?" Dalia asked.

"*Tres* tacky, if you ask me," Hal said jokingly. Dalia punched Hal's shoulder and put on her sad puppy face. Hal ignored her.

"Susie was talking to me this morning. She said, 'Gerry is just so cool! I mean, won't his Bar Mitzvah be a blast? Whoops! Totally didn't mean to rub it in 'cause you aren't going, Hal!' I just wanted to punch her!" Hal yelled, stomping her feet.

"Just you wait. Robby and I have it *all* covered!" Dalia whispered, smiling.

When the two girls reached their school, P.S. 129, they stood on the concrete steps and got in a huddle. Soon, Robby appeared from across the street. Robby was their best friend also. Even though he could sometimes be a bit of a snob, he was still nice.

"So, girls. How's it going? Are Evil McEvil and Totally Gross here?" Robby said.

Hal and Dalia laughed, understanding the inside joke. Evil McEvil and Totally Gross were the nicknames for Mallory and Susie.

"Yes. The two 'unnamed-soon-to-be-victims' should be coming up in the Mercedes Benz in a second," Dalia whispered. Sure enough, soon the two twins stepped out of Gloria's black Mercedes and walked up towards the steps of P.S. 129, AKA Howard Johnson Junior High.

"Aren't these silk skirts fab, Halleywood?" Susie stated coldly. Halleywood was Hal's nickname since she had always wanted to be an actress in Los Angeles.

"More like, 'Aren't these silk skirts fat-looking," Dalia mumbled.

Robby looked at the girls and gave them a wink. In a way, he could look like Leonardo DeCaprio, only with red hair. The evil twins were almost in love with him.

"I think they look…fine. Here, hold on. You have something on your face." Robby began. Then, he pulled out a pack of hand wipes. Apparently, Robby had told them they had something on their faces. When Mallory and Susie wiped their faces, their faces turned red. Then they screamed. Dalia and Robby burst out laughing. Hal sighed.

"YOU DIDN'T TELL US THAT THESE WET WIPES WOULD BURN OUR FACES!" Susie yelled, stomping her feet and trying to slap Robby.

Then Dalia got her water bottle and squirted it all over the twins' silk skirts. Apparently, her water bottle had been filled up with red Koolaid.

Hal took Robby and Dalia's arms and tugged them into school. The bell must have rung five minutes ago or so, because no one was outside except for the Safety Patrolman and an old teacher who was drawing something in his notebook.

When Hal walked home, she had no one to talk to. She had been disappointed in Robby and Dalia for getting on the evil twin's level of awfulness. She talked to both of her friends at lunch and, of course, Dalia got upset and Robby defended himself. So, Hal was on her own. When she reached the front door for her home, she walked inside and heard a yell. Mallory ran towards Hal and started hitting her with a tin of Pringles. Hal guarded her sore spot on her arm, where she had fallen last week. Then Hal managed to run to her room and lock her door.

"Well, well, well. I've been waiting for you!" Susie said mysteriously.

Hal turned around and sighed. "Get away! I didn't do anything!" Hal yelled.

Susie got up and moaned. She bit her lip and looked towards the door. "Mommy! MOMMY! Hal is being mean!" Susie yelled.

Gloria came upstairs and was alarmed when Hal's door was locked. Susie unlocked the door and pushed Hal aside. Susie lay on the ground. Gloria began yelling at Hal.

Hal couldn't hear it though. She was running downstairs, into the elevator, down and out of the apartment building. She stood on the streets of her hometown in New York and sighed. What was up with her stepsisters? Couldn't they see that Hal had done nothing? Hal walked down the street and passed a bunch of people who were coming home. Her whole life appeared strange because it seemed a bit like a movie she had seen once. Wasn't it called Cinderella?

"Sorry. She's out with Robby," Dalia's mom said. Hal had walked towards Dalia's house and wanted to talk to Dalia and complain. Dalia would just make Hal some hot chocolate and tell her nice things. But Hal forgot that the two of them were in a fight.

"Ok. Thanks Mrs. Bernard," Hal said quietly turning back towards the street.

Hal walked back to her apartment building and crept towards her room. She noticed that Gloria, Mallory, and Susie were asleep in the living room. Hal lay back on her bed and shut her eyes.

When Hal woke up, everything seemed to be the same. It was just a typical Saturday morning. Hal walked downstairs and looked towards the fridge. She saw leftovers from Chang Mow Ling's Chinese and Japanese restaurant.

"Mmm…This will be good! Wasabi and tuna rolls. Interesting," Hal whispered sarcastically, sniffing the plastic box that sat on the counter. Hal began eating the spicy tuna rolls that were sure to clean her sinuses. When she had eventually eaten all of her unusual breakfast, she set off to her bedroom. Darn, her bathroom was flooded again. Hal gently walked up the stairs, down the hall, and past two doors. She opened the large, white, wooden door that stood before her. She was entering a danger zone, otherwise known as Susie's bedroom. Susie, Mallory, and Gloria were out shopping for dresses for Gerry's Bar Mitzvah. Hal looked around Susie's room and was in awe. It was beautiful and pink and everything was piled up with fluff and tons of silky lace. The floor was white wood covered with tons of plush rugs. Hal tiptoed over to the door of Susie's bathroom and opened it. She turned on the bathtub's handle and began pouring in a large tube of pink bubble bath. When the tub was filled with water and wonderful, large bubbles, Hal jumped in and laughed. This was fun! Hal began falling asleep as she sat in the bathtub, soaking up the wonderfulness and warmness that she had never known before. She rarely took baths, only showers, and even then the water in her shower was cold and smelled awful.

"What is she doing in here, Mother? I come in, just wanting to comb my hair and here is 'Queen of the World' sitting in *my* bathtub! Can't I get *any* privacy in my own *house*? Mother, straighten this girl OUT!" Susie screamed, creating a fuss.

Hal stood up from the bathtub and wrapped a soft towel around her. She ran out of Susie's bathroom and into her own. Soon, she was getting dressed and hiding from her stepmother.

"That's it! I have had enough of you! Stay here! You cannot go out! Definitely not to the Bar

Mitzvah! Gerry will only have eyes for my daughters, not you…you, you…filthy, dirty, step-daughter!" Gloria yelled as she walked into Hal's bedroom.

Then, looking mighty satisfied; the two stepsisters walked in and cackled along with Gloria. The stepsisters were dressed from head to toe with designer fashions. Mallory wore a white mini dress paired with black clogs and a leather jacket. Susie wore tight fitting jeans, a small shirt, and big high heels. Maybe Gloria was right. Maybe Gerry would only have eyes for Mallory and Susie.

Hal sat on the stone bench in the garden that was placed on top of her apartment's deck. Even though it was on the 23rd floor, it was amazing to go to and see the over-watered and over-colored flowers. Hal started crying, thinking of the amazing fun that Susie, Gloria, and Mallory were having right now. As soon as the girl's first teardrop landed on the floor, a small bubble floated down from the sky. Then, more floated down and, finally, a big bubble burst open. Out came a small, chubby lady who looked like a queen. She had ruby red lips, a tight black dress, and her gray hair in a tight bun.

"What is wrong, little Hal? Are you ok? What is wrong, little Hal? Is there a bad case of tooth decay? I can fix it! I have a wand… I can fix it; I'll make you look like a swan! Are you ok, Little Hal? Has it been a long day? Are the sisters acting up, soon to disappear like the last sunray?" the women began singing.

This magic woman intrigued Hal. She sang beautiful songs that made Hal feel sleepy.

"Who are you?" Hal asked, looking up toward the woman.

"I am your Fairy Godmother, poppet…," the lady said quietly.

"Really, then? If you're magic, get me a pink lemonade!" Hal demanded.

Soon, a big glass of lemonade sat down on Hal's lap and Hal jumped up.

"See, I told you! Now, what do you want? I saw you cry," the Godmother said.

"You are magic! Wow! This is just like Cinderella! Hey, you

know what? You could do something for me. I was crying because I can't go to this really nice boy's Bar Mitzvah because I got in trouble and then I got in even more trouble! I need a dress, a hairdo, maybe even a limo to deliver me to the party!" Hal whispered.

"Ok, walk inside to your bedroom and there will sit a beautiful outfit, shoes included, a phone number for a salon, and six small men. If you feed the men three eggs each, throw them out the window and walk downstairs...There will be a limo! Now go, and be warned. If you aren't back by 12 in the morning, you return to normal," the Fairy murmured, patting Hal on the back. Then, she disappeared just as quickly as she had come.

Hal ran inside, closing the door to the porch. She walked excitedly into her bedroom and there sat the most gorgeous outfit in the world. There was a white, short sleeved shirt that was tight and felt like silk. It was paired with a black mini skirt and black high heels. Hal put the outfit on and grabbed the card for the salon. She called the number and was told that the stylist would be over in five minutes. Then, she took the six small men and fed them three eggs each. Hal tossed them out the window and then opened the door to the stylist. Within 30 minutes, her hair was done up in a beautiful messy-bun that was held together with two chopsticks. Hal walked downstairs and helped the stylist into her pink van. Then, she looked over to the limo. It was big and black and expensive looking. Hal stepped in and told the driver where to drive. Wow, happily ever after might exist. At least, tonight it would.

Later, the limousine reached Gerry's house. It was a huge mansion that had a big gate wrapped around it. Hal got out of the limo and thanked the driver. She walked up to the front gate and said, "Party Guest, invitation number 3319." The gate opened and Hal walked up to the house, looking around at all of the people. She saw Robby and Dalia who smiled and waved, surprising enough.

"Sorry we did that to your evil step-sisters. But I have to admit, it was hysterical!" Robby said, looking over at Hal.

Hal smiled and hugged both of her friends. Then, the evil twins arrived. Susie and Mallory walked over to Hal and grimaced.

"You look familiar…" Susie yelled, looking at Hal's face.

"Oh…Well, ok! Yeah. You don't know m," Hal said, getting embarrassed. She didn't want the twins to find out that she was there.

Then, Gerry walked over. It was Gerry's party and he was getting to know his guests, supposedly. Gerry looked like a Prince with his fancy tuxedo and hairdo. "Hello, why don't I know *you?*" Gerry said to Hal.

Hal blushed and then looked at the twins. Both of them were bright red. Dalia and Robby walked over to the snack bar and Gerry invited Hal to dance.

So, it turns out that Gerry is a really nice guy. His parents wanted him to have a big party since he was turning 13 and so he invited most of the kids in his grade. That included Hal, Dalia, Robby, etc. Gerry and Hal spent the rest of the party together, dancing and talking about school. Except, at 11:58, Hal had to escape.

"So, what's your name, dear?" Gerry asked.

"You don't know me…I'm some…big geek," Hal whispered.

Gerry looked like he was about to speak, but then Hal noticed the time.

"Here, IM me at ArcticIceCaps183! I have to go!" Hal yelled. Hal ran from the house and then turned back to normal. She was dressed in her ragged jeans and blank red shirt. She ran down the street and fell when she tripped on a rock. Then, she got up again and ran all the way back home. The first thing she did was make sure that she had checked her Instant Messages. Then, she went to sleep.

"How was the party?" Hal asked at breakfast.

"Good, but there was some gorgeous girl there who stole Gerry's heart! She looked just like you, only pretty," Mallory replied blankly.

Hal made a face and finished her toast. If only Gerry knew that she was the girl. But she couldn't tell him. He was different, wealthy…popular.

"Miss U. What's up? What's ur name?" The instant message said.

Hal had been on her computer doing homework when she realized that she had a message. She had checked it and it had been from LonelyHeart5580, AKA Gerry.

"Ur party was nice. C u l8tr." Hal replied, looking at her computer screen. She missed him, and she knew it. Hal got up from her desk and walked outside. She was going to Gerry's house. She would tell him she was the one. Then, Gloria stopped her.

"Get back in here! Back in, NOW! Gerry is coming around to see who his 'girl' is! She left a black high heel!" Gloria yelled, pushing Hal into a closet. She locked the closet.

Hal was so upset. It was she! It was she who lost the shoe! Hal began unlocking the door.

The stepsisters were trying on the shoe when Hal burst out through the closet.

"Mother, you were supposed to lock her up!" Susie yelled.

"But…but…but," Gloria began.

"MY DREAMS!" Mallory yelled.

"MY MONEY!" Susie shrieked.

"My princess?!" Gerry bellowed.

Hal jumped up to the couch and tried the shoe on. It fit perfectly. Susie, Mallory, and Gloria began crying as Gerry hugged Hal. That's when Hal noticed that her Fairy Godmother was sitting in a cabinet, looking out and grinning, ear to ear.

Now Hal lives with her Fairy Godmother. Gloria was found cheating on the stock market and convicted to life in prison.

Fantasy

Mary Biggs
Jacob Brakebill
Sarah Matlock
Michael Sproat

The Dragon Scale

Mary Biggs

"The dragons approached from over the horizon, growing nearer and nearer with every step. The villagers screamed! And then……."

Bridget put down the pages that she had been reading out loud to her friend Melissa and sighed.

"What happened?!" asked Melissa. "What do the villagers do?"

"I don't know," answered Bridget. "I can't think anymore."

"But you've got to finish your story," said Melissa. "I won't sleep if you don't!"

"Hahaha, very funny 'Lissa," said Bridget. "I'll think about it over the weekend. See you Monday." And with that, she picked up her pages, stuffed them in her backpack, and walked away.

"See you Monday, and good luck!" called Melissa after Bridget's retreating back.

"Thanks 'Lissa," called Bridget over her shoulder, then walked out of sight.

That night, Bridget was still no closer to finishing her story. In her desperation, she even asked her older sister, Rose, to help her. Rose replied like she always did.

"Don't bother me now, I'm doing homework." Just like always.

"I swear, she must be the smartest person in Pinewood High," thought Bridget. Aloud, she said, "I need help with my story."

"You mean that stupid little thing about dragons and villages?" asked Rose. "I'm surprised that you haven't asked me before now."

"It is not a stupid little thing!" yelled back Bridget, turning, as she so often did, every one of her sister's comments into an argument. "It's better then any story that you ever wrote."

"Is not!" flared Rose.

"Girls! Calm down!" came their mother's voice from downstairs.

Bridget and Rose looked at each other. When their mom used that voice, it ment that arguing was over for the day. Rose went back to her homework, and Bridget tiptoed out.

Even when she was in bed, Bridget couldn't stop thinking about her story.

"The villagers screamed, and then…" she murmured over and over. Several times, she jumped out of bed, grabbed a piece of paper, and jotted down an idea or two, then scowled and ripped up the paper.

Finally, she threw herself back on her bed and heaved a deep sigh.

"I can't do it," Bridget told herself. "Just stop thinking about it. Melissa will just have to make up her own ending."

But somehow, the story would not leave Bridget's mind. Even while she was drifting off to sleep, she was still murmuring, "The dragons appeared over the horizon…"

Bridget woke with a start, and looked around in wonder. She was definitely not in her room anymore, but where was she?

All around her was greenness. Green trees, green grass, green scales…green scales?!

Bridget sat straight up, and scrambled over to where something lay shimmering in the grass. She looked at them with wonder. They couldn't be what she thought they were, but what else could they be?

"They are," Bridget whispered, "dragon scales."

She picked one up, and turned it around in her hands. It was smooth and cool, and felt kind of rough, like snakeskin.

"And if there are dragon scales," she reasoned with herself, "there must be dragons somewhere."

No sooner had Bridget said that than a shadow fell over her. She looked up and gasped. Standing over her was a dragon. It was about seven feet tall and had blue and silver scales. The dragon was staring at her quizzically, and making soft grunting noises in its throat. Bridget got the feeling that the dragon wanted to say something, but just couldn't quite get it out.

"Hello," said Bridget, her voice breaking through the stillness that had begun when the dragon appeared. "Who are you?"

As soon as she said it, Bridget realized what a stupid question it was if the dragon couldn't answer. But then, the dragon grunted and began waving its hands around, then walked a couple feet and looked back at her expectantly. Bridget realized that it wanted her to follow, so gathering all the courage she could muster, she put down the dragon scale, which she had been clutching, and followed the dragon out of the meadow.

They walked over the grassy meadows with the dragon taking long strides forward, then stopping every few minutes to look behind it and wait for Bridget to catch up. Since the dragon took two strides in the same amount of time Bridget took four, Bridget was getting kind of tired, and when the dragon finally stopped before a long strip of weeping willow trees, she sank down on the ground to rest.

The dragon went up to the trees and made a soft, low, purring sound, much like the one it had used for Bridget in the meadow, except this was lower and longer. Then, as the tired girl looked on in amazement, the willow trees parted silently, and out stepped a huge dragon. It was three times bigger and taller then the little dragon that Bridget had met, and its scales shimmered a deep forest green.

The newcomer spoke to the little dragon in tones of reprimand, not noticing Bridget, who was still on the ground. Finally, the little dragon said one last thing and pointed at the girl that he had brought. The big dragon finally noticed.

"Who are you?" the sound of the words echoed inside Bridget's head, though she was sure she hadn't thought of them. She looked around frantically. "Who are you?" There was the voice again, and Bridget realized with shock that it was the big dragon that was talking to her!

"I am Bridget Matthews, and how can you talk to me?" Bridget answered.

"Well it's obvious that you believe in us dragons," said the big dragon. "I mean, you're writing a story about us!"

"Well, yes I am," said Bridget. "I mean I was."

"Was?" inquired the dragon.

"Qurrrrrrr?" said the little dragon, which Bridget guessed must mean the same thing.

"Yes. You see, I kind of got writer's block halfway through, and now I can't think of how the story should continue." Answered Bridget

"Well maybe you should come and see the king dragon," said the big dragon. "He can probably help you." And with those words, he turned around and pushed through the thick leaves of the trees. Bridget, not knowing what else to do, followed, with the little dragon peering after her. Bridget got the feeling that the little dragon wanted nothing more than to follow her, but that he was not allowed.

"I'll be back out soon," said Bridget to her little friend, before letting the boughs drop behind her.

Once inside, she stopped short. Right in front of her eyes the whole clearing had turned into a grand hall, much like the ones in old medieval castles, except this hall was draped with even finer tapestries, and the floor was carpeted with shimmering green scales that the dragons had shed. The ceiling was all blue and gold, more scales from different colored dragons. The hall was packed with dragons, each one a different size, shape, or color from his neighbor. They were all talking when Bridget came in, but as soon as she entered, there was an intense silence, and all the dragons looked at her.

The big dragon stopped, turned around, and beckoned to Bridget, who was standing stunned at the doorway.

"It's alright," he said reassuringly. "You'll get use to them soon. Come on."

Bridget found that her feet could move again, and followed, self-conscious amid the stares of the dragons, the big dragon to the front of the room. Seated on a huge throne made of pure gold was the biggest dragon Bridget had seen yet. Its scales were every color of the rainbow, and glittered with a fiery sheen that Bridget had only once before seen, when there had been a hard frost, and the whole world sparkled.

"What?" Bridget was jogged out of her memory when she realized the dragon had spoken to her. "I'm sorry I didn't hear you."

" I said, welcome to our land. Where have you come from?" answered the dragon.

"Thank you," said Bridget, then, as her guide shot her a look, accented it with a small curtsy. "I don't know how I got here, but I came from New York."

"Where is New York?" asked the dragon.

"In North America," Bridget answered.

"And you have come to our land in search of what?"

"Well, I sort of came here by mistake, but now that I'm here, I would like to have a tour," said

Bridget. "And I would also like to find out more about you dragons."

"Greenstone. Come here." This remark was directed at the green dragon that had brought Bridget. He stepped forward and bowed. "Map out a tour of our land for the young lady and get together a group to accompany her. That should take about one day. Tomorrow, they will set off, and be back in time for the full moon, which is the only time she can get back." Greenstone bowed and departed, and the king turned his attention to Bridget. "While we are waiting for him to finish, you must have a room. I will fix one up for you for tonight, but for right now, go back out side and meet the little dragons. They are very anxious to meet you. We will send for you at dinner time."

Bridget curtsied again and turned around to find that she did not know the way out! Fortunately, a sea blue dragon noticed her confusion and came up to her.

"I am Sea Morning," she introduced herself. "I can see that you are confused. Can I help?"

"I am Bridget Matthews. Nice to meet you," Bridget said. "Would you be kind enough to show me the way out?"

"Yes I would," Sea Morning said with a laugh like bells ringing. "Just turn to the left and go in an exactly straight line and you can't miss the door."

"Thank you very much," said Bridget, and started in the direction the dragon had pointed. In a short time she saw the door, and pushed through it into the bright, sunny afternoon.

The little dragon was still waiting for her, and made a glad sound when Bridget came out.

"I told you I would come back," laughed Bridget as she patted it on the head. "I wonder what your name is?"

" Sea Star," said a voice from behind. Bridget whipped around with a gasp to find a pearly gray dragon watching her with amusement.

"Excuse me, but I didn't see you there," Bridget said with a laugh.

"Quite all right," answered the dragon. "I find I have a talent for sneaking up on people! Anyway, in answer to your question, this little guy's name is Sea Star."

"Thank you," said Bridget. "Who are you?"

"My full name is Mist in the Morning, but folks just call me Misty. I am Sea Star's big sister."

"Oh!" said Bridget with surprise. "Does he have any more siblings?"

"Nope, just me," said Misty with a laugh.

"How come I can talk to you and Greenstone and the king, but not to Sea Star?" asked Bridget.

"Well, you see, dragons have to be a certain age before they can communicate with other species. It didn't used to be like that, but about a hundred years ago a wizard came to our valley and almost destroyed the entire population!"

"How?" asked Bridget, intrigued with the story.

"He made a deal with a young dragon," Misty said with a sigh. "That wizard said he would get the little dragon all the jewels that she could wish for if she would tell him where the sacred opal was."

"And?" breathed Bridget.

"She told him," said Misty with a dry smile. "Once he had that information, there was absolutely nothing stopping him from doing anything he wanted, and if the king hadn't found out about it, I wouldn't be here right now telling you all this."

"How do you know it?" asked Bridget.

"I was the little dragon," answered Misty with a glance at Bridget.

"Oh I see," Bridget thought for a few minutes. "Then how old will Sea Star have to be before he can talk to me?"

"Oh, about a hundred years or so," said Misty with an airy wave of her hand. "I just turned one hundred two last week."

Bridget drew back, partly in surprise, and partly because the little dragon had gotten impatient with no attention coming to him, had pulled on her shirt, and was now sucking the back of it very happily. If attention was what he wanted, the little dragon got his wish.

"Why you little scamp!" cried Bridget with a laugh as she

tried to wrestle her shirt away from him.

Misty laughed. "He has the family trait of doing things unexpectedly!"

When Bridget had finally gotten her shirt away from the sharp little jaws of Sea Star, she sat down on the ground to play with him a little bit. Misty watched them in amusement, then quietly tip toed away.

All to soon, it was getting dark, and another dragon came up to inform Bridget that her room was ready for her, and that her dinner was ready too.

"Good-bye 'till tomorrow!" Bridget told Sea Star, and followed the dragon inside.

The next morning Bridget woke up early, but found that the dragons had been up even earlier, for on the table in the middle of the room was a hearty breakfast of eggs, bacon, and delicious pancakes. There was also a silvery looking liquid in a silver goblet that Bridget guessed must be some sort of dragon version of orange juice.

As Bridget was finishing breakfast, the dragon that had informed Bridget her room was ready the night before came in and set down a small suitcase.

"You may pack in this," she said, then without explaining further, stepped out of the room and closed the door behind her.

As the door was closing, it swung open again and in stepped Greenstone.

"Did you find every thing all right?" he asked.

"Oh yes the room is very comfortable, and the breakfast was great," Bridget said with enthusiasm. "But what was the stuff in the goblet?"

"That was Kukundora, the thing we dragons drink to make sure our scales stay clean," replied Greenstone after Bridget showed him the drink. " I'm sorry you got one on your tray. Things are hectic in the kitchen today, what with all the last minute preparations for our trip today."

"Oh so that's what she meant!" exclaimed Bridget, and told Greenstone about the dragon who had given her the suitcase. "Who is she anyway? And what does she think I have to pack?"

"That is Ruby-stone," Greenstone informed Bridget. "She is the palace maid. As for what do you have to pack, what about clothes, books, journals, and all that?"

"But I don't have that stuff here!" exclaimed Bridget. "I have all of it at home, but I didn't bring anything."

"Look in your closet," said Greenstone with a twinkle in his eye.

Bridget, not knowing what else to do, followed his instructions and was amazed at the bounty she found. In her closet were at least five dresses that all fit perfectly, three books, one about the history of dragons, one of the dragon language, and one a book of maps that had every single area of dragon land covered. Bridget couldn't have asked for more, but something in Greenstone's eyes told her to look again, and there in the back of the closet was a blank book that was titled: Bridget's Dragon Kingdom Record.

"Oh thank you so much!" Bridget exclaimed happily.

"We will set off at 10:00 sharp, so be ready," Greenstone told Bridget. "Come down as soon as you are finished packing." Then he went out the door.

At 9:55, Bridget was done with her packing. In her suitcase were all three books from the closet, and the journal, though she doubted that she would have enough time to write in it. She had also changed out of her nightshirt (which she had been wearing when she went to sleep and had left on) and put on one of the dresses from the closet. She would have preferred jeans and a regular shirt, but there were none in her closet.

Just as Bridget closed her suitcase, Ruby-stone came hurrying in.

"The escort is ready to leave whenever you are," she told Bridget with a hurried smile. "I told them you would be right down."

"Thank you," replied Bridget. "I am ready to go now. Just finished packing, actually!"

“Then hurry!” said the dragon-maid with a frazzled laugh.

“Are you alright?” inquired Bridget. “You see kind of jumpy.”

“Everyone is getting ready for the festival of the full moon in seven days,” answered Ruby-stone. “It is the biggest festival of the year.”

“Why is it so special?” asked Bridget again, and added, as Ruby-stone shot her a warning look, “I will go down after this.”

“The reason is that this is the only time of the year when we dragons can fly out of our own land,” said Ruby-stone with a dreamy look in her eyes. “It is also the only time that we can visit with the Spirit of All Dragons.”

“Oh I see,” said Bridget. “But why can’t dragons fly out of their own land the rest of the year?”

Ruby-stone turned from making Bridget’s bed, and fixed her with a hard stare that would have melted ice.

“All right, all right, I’m going now!” exclaimed Bridget, and with these words, she grabbed her suitcase and ran out of the room. Ruby-stone looked after her with an amused glance, then turned back around, and continued with her morning chores.

The day was bright and sunny, and a perfect day for traveling. Bridget paused only to say a quick good morning to a red-gold dragon clearing up dragon-sized leftovers from the dragon's own breakfast. Then, she ran outside.

And stopped in amazement for the second time in two days.

There, before her, was a crowd of even more dragons then had been at the party the night before. They were ranged in rows from largest to smallest, the front row being the smallest (the littlest one was 6 feet tall), and the last row consisting of huge dragons, the largest being over twelve feet in height. Even the king was standing in the multi-colored crowd.

As Bridget stood there, speechless, (the reflections of the sun on scales was beginning to hurt her eyes) a trumpet blared from out of nowhere, and all the dragons turned to face Bridget.

"Come forward," said a deep voice inside her head. "Get onto the horse."

As if on cue, a beautiful mare stepped out from between the dragon rows. The horse was a pure, unbroken black, except for on her withers. There, a white mark in the shape of a dragon displayed itself and even shimmered with a scale-like sheen.

It was the most amazing sight Bridget had ever seen, and her attention was immediately distracted from the dragons, and riveted on the horse.

"Get onto the horse," the deep voice commanded again, and Bridget obeyed.

Although she had never ridden before, the girl and the horse seemed to belong together, and Bridget felt calm.

"Move out!" Another voice erupted inside Bridget's head, and as one, all the dragons began to move out toward the open field. The horse followed, and Bridget found that it moved with a lovely, slow, rocking motion that reminded the girl in some way of morning mist on the waters of a lake.

"I will name you Mist on the Lake," Bridget whispered to the gentle horse beneath her. "Lake for short."

The newly christened horse tossed her head as if agreeing to the name.

If Bridget had thought that all of the dragons that had been outside the castle were to come on the journey with her, she was mistaken. Nearly all of them stopped short (for no reason that Bridget could see) after the procession had been walking for about five minutes, and only a few kept on going. Bridget was glad to see that Greenstone, Sea Morning, and Mist in the Morning were among the dragons that stayed. She was even happier when Sea Star galloped up behind her and started trotting alongside Lake as she walked with Bridget on her. The group only looked back once to wave good-bye to the remaining dragons.

After what seemed like hours to Bridget but was probably only about one or two, Greenstone, who seemed to be the leader, called a halt for a morning break. The dragons found a nice little shady place beneath a few large trees, and started to set up a picnic. Bridget slid off Lake, who immediately began to crop the grass that was growing in plenty as far as the eye could see.

When the dragons sat down for lunch, Bridget sat down next to Mist in the Morning and took the basket that was offered to her. She looked inside and discovered a delicious lunch of bread, fruit that she had never seen before but that was marvelous, a cold drink that was copper but quite tasty and filling, and last of all, a pan of fudge that was the best Bridget had ever tasted.

As the girl ate, she looked at the dragon she was sitting by and wondering if it would be polite to ask Misty a question. Misty decided for her by turning to smile at her and saying "So what do you want to ask me?"

Bridget was embarrassed that Misty should catch her staring, but decided to take advantage of the dragon's offer.

"I was talking to Ruby-stone this morning," Bridget began timidly.

"And...," prodded Misty when Bridget paused, "go on."

"Well, we got on the subject of the festival of the full moon, and when she was describing it, she said something that did not make sense." Bridget continued, reassured by the smile on Misty's face.

"What was it?" asked Misty gently.

"That you dragons could not fly out of your own country except on the night of the festival." Bridget was speaking more quickly now, and not thinking about what she was saying. So she blurted out: "Does that have something to do with the deal you made with the wizard?"

Bridget blushed as the dragon laughed.

"Yes it does," Misty answered with a last chuckle. "In fact, that is the only thing that the wizard did before the king found out and destroyed him. That is why we have the festival of the moon every year: to visit with the humans that we used to visit regularly."

"I get it now," said Bridget with a satisfied smile. "Thank you."

"No problem," replied Misty with a grin. "And it is a good thing you get it, because it is time to move on."

For the rest of that day, Bridget rode among the dragons, introducing herself and making new friends. But she always stayed with the dragon she had met first, because even though they couldn't talk, the two could still communicate, and did so almost non-stop. Sea Star was also the one to start to point out important landmarks for Bridget. She would then go over to one of the dragons that she could communicate with and ask them to tell her more about the place of interest. Or, if every one was in conversation with another, Bridget simply looked in her dragon history book, or saved it to ask Misty or Sea Morning or Greenstone or one of her other new friends about when Greenstone called a rest.

The next two days were similar to the first one. Very similar.

In fact, the temperature and weather didn't change at all.

Bridget mentioned this to one of her new friends, a middle aged dragon called Goldstar, because he was a green dragon, but on his forehead blossomed a shimmering star of golden scales.

"The weather is always like this in the week leading up to the Festival," he replied in answer to her question. Bridget had discovered that all the dragons she talked to pronounced the word festival as if it had a capital "F" starting it. She didn't know why it sounded like that to her, but it indisputably did.

"But why?" Bridget had never asked that question as much as she had in the past four days.

"Because everyone needs to prepare for the celebrations, and they can't do it right if the weather is rainy," said Goldstar.

Her curiosity satisfied for the moment, Bridget rode back to her place beside Sea Star.

The third day was when things started to happen.

That morning, the little group had set off without mishap, but everyone was feeling uneasy. The very *air* seemed to tingle with magic, and Lake was too jittery for Bridget to feel entirely comfortable. Her suspicions were confirmed that afternoon when Peacock (Greenstone's little brother) sat down and refused to go any farther. Since his brother could usually sense bad magic, Greenstone called a halt, and went off with his brother to learn why Peacock was so afraid.

While they were talking, Sea Morning came up to Bridget.

"I am very uneasy," she confided to Bridget with a nervous sigh. "Something is going to happen, I just know it."

"Lake thinks so too." Bridget's horse had been jumpy all afternoon, and when one of the dragons riding near Bridget had swatted at a fly, Lake had nearly bucked her rider off, so high strung was she.

The dragons were anxiously waiting for their leader's verdict, and they all tensed when he came out of the shade of a willow tree where he had been conferring with his brother.

"Elf magic." That was all Greenstone said, but all of the dragons seemed to know what he meant, and all let out a big sigh.

"I thought as much!" a burly dragon named Garnet shouted. This remark prompted more just like it. Bridget and Sea Star huddled in the back until Greenstone called the dragons back to order.

"I am as distressed as you are that the elves are wrecking havoc again, but since we have a guest, (he gestured toward Bridget) we will not fight unless they directly attack us. Is that clear?"

Greenstone looked around at the group, catching each dragon's eye individually until he was sure that everyone understood him. Then, he continued, "We will go on as usual and continue our trip. Move out!"

Without another word, the dragons got into their formations, and continued on the journey.

The next day, the feel of magic was stronger then ever, and the dragons whispered that the elves could not be far away, and that maybe they should send out war parties. However, Greenstone somehow managed to uncover all of the schemes, and squashed every one. There was little he could do that afternoon, though, for as the dragons were passing through a forest, wild war cries came searing through the stillness.

Greenstone immediately started shouting out orders, and the dragons formed themselves into a line. In the midst of all the excitement, Bridget didn't know what to do. So she backed up into the edges of the skirmish and concealed herself beneath a huge weeping willow. She would have to ask Goldstar or one of the others why the dragons and the elves hated each other so much.

Elves were dropping from the trees and onto the dragons. Neither party had weapons of any sort, which was fortunate, although both sides would have been evenly matched.

The elves, though trained in hand-to-hand combat, had no training in strategy, and although they outnumbered the dragons, elves don't have the dragon's gift of blowing fire, which these dragons were doing constantly. The dragons numbered fewer then the elves, but they had better strategies.

Bridget was content to watch, until an elf approached Sea Star from behind. No one saw him as he crept toward Sea Star's unprotected back. No one except Bridget. She was watching in horror as he approached her friend, her mind filled with thoughts of what the dragon kingdom would be like without her young friend there to amuse her and play with her and "talk" with her. The thought was horrible.

Suddenly, as the elf neared Sea Star, Bridget discovered that she was shaking. Not in fright, not in sadness, but in anger. And she couldn't remember ever being this angry.

How dare this elf try to kill her friend? He had no right! And the dragons had been so kind to Bridget when they could've very well eaten her.

When she thought about it, Bridget discovered that she owed all that to Sea Star. He might not have found her, and another, more hostile dragon might have found her instead. And now an elf was probably going to kill him.

Bridget decided to act, just like the heroines in books. But unlike them, she did not have any weapons to use and no magic experience. Bridget looked frantically around and saw only one branch off of the tree. She picked it up, and kicked Lake into a gallop.

The elf was almost on Sea Star, and still no one had seen him. Bridget rode hard, and when she was within striking distance, she threw the branch with all her strength.

It got nowhere near the elf, and Bridget gasped in fury. Fortunately, the sound of something whizzing by his ear distracted the elf from his target, and as he turned in surprise, Sea Star finally saw him.

With a yell of fury, the young dragon let loose a burst of orange flame, and the elf that had tried to kill him was gone.

The dragons were victorious, and the last few days of the journey continued without event. Bridget was, however, given some of the dragon's magic to use for the rest of her stay, in case elves gave them trouble again. None did.

On the morning of the group's departure, Bridget felt a twinge of sadness. She was nearing the end of her stay, and she felt forlorn as she brushed Lake.

Her friends noticed and made sure that the ride home was lively and fun for Bridget. Greenstone even ordered a detour so she could see where the sacred opal was kept. She couldn't see it of course, but that was all right, because the dragons promised that she would see it at the Festival.

So the ride home was happy.

When the dragons and Bridget returned to the castle, they found that it had been set upon by a band of elves. Fortunately, they were easy to deal with, and Greenstone did so in only two hours.

The full moon was shining brightly as Bridget came down from her room, dressed in a silver dress with a pattern like dragon scales. The palace was deserted as she walked out into the moonlit air that seemed to glow.

"You will stay for the first part of the Festival," Greenstone's familiar voice rang through her head. "Then we will get someone to take you home."

"Ok. How soon will that be?"

"In about 15 minutes." Greenstone settled himself beside her. "The fireworks will start in a few moments.

They did, beautiful, shooting bursts of light and color. Their brightness was almost hypnotizing Bridget, and she was nearly asleep. She jerked awake just in time to see the sacred opal, then drowsed off again. Bridget was drifting off into sleep, and something told her that she was going home.

"Bye Greenstone, Goldstar, Sea Morning, Misty, and…," Bridget smiled in her sleep, "bye Sea Star.

She was vaguely aware that all her friends were around her, whispering, but Bridget was too sleepy to care. The last thing she heard was Sea Star, purring.

"Wow! Is this a great story or what?!" Melissa exclaimed as she read the last line. "I'm glad you decided to change the topic from dragons being bad, to dragons fighting elves. And you write so convincingly! It almost seems as if you were there yourself!"

Bridget only smiled, reached into her pocket, and fingered the dragon scale she had found under her pillow when she woke up after visiting the dragons. Lying in bed, it had seemed like a fantastic dream, until Bridget put her nightshirt under her pillow. There, she found a single dragon scale that glimmered with all the colors of her friends. And in the center of the scale was a star, glowing sea colored.

Bridget had jumped out of bed and worked on a new story for the rest of the weekend. Now, Monday, 'Lissa liked her story, and thought it sounded like she was there herself!

As Melissa walked ahead, Bridget paused and drew the scale out of her pocket. The star reflected the sunshine, and in her light-blinded eyes, Bridget saw Sea Star, purring and frolicking.

Bridget smiled, stuck the scale back into her pocket, and ran to catch up with her friend.

Merlin's Return: A Continuation of King Arthur (with acknowledgment to J.R.R. Tolkein)

Part One

Jacob Brakebill

Ten years after Arthur's death, Merlin was released from the cave he was sealed into. Three knights known by King Arthur carefully guarded his work. They were Sirs Lancelot, Galahad, and Gawain. One day, Merlin accidentally turned them into a chimera, a roc, and a phoenix. Then Merlin got an idea. "I will change you back if bring me the Pyramid of Excalibur."

They had no choice but to accept. "One piece is in Morgan le Fay's fortress. One is in The Black Knight's manor. One is in the Red Knight's manor. All three are feared places, especially the first. The guards are evil, giant beings. They formerly guarded the Holy Grail. I know the secret to beating them!" said Sir Galahad.

They left for the Red Knight's manor. They slew foes till the Chimera dropped dead. They won the "The Pyramid of Life." It revives all dead allies, including King Arthur!

Arthur knew his knight's even as mythical beasts.

Part 2

King Arthur had a mythical sword that orcs called "Stabber" and goblins called "Smasher." But men called it "Excalibur." Hobbits have no name for it.

Let me tell you about hobbits. They are fat. They take as long as they want. I wouldn't blame you if you hated them.

This part of the story started in Bashville.* The four heroes had walked to the village when a hunting party of hobbits ambushed them. King Arthur drew his blade. Each hobbit had a shotgun. The knights were able to change shape from animal to human. So, they beat the hobbits and fled the village. The hobbits joined them.

Together, they searched for the second pyramid piece. They were in the Black Knight's manor. The "Pyramid of Doom" was found by a hobbit.

But another force was at work here. Morgan le Fay had joined the fight. She was waiting them at her fortress. On the way to Morgan le Fay's fortress, they stopped in a village and learned a terrible secret. One hundred thousand orcs are getting ready for war! There are not enough soldiers in the armies of old.

"We shall send word to dwarf and to the elf. They are our only allies, except for Eagles and Ents. They will help us. I must head to

Merlin's tower at the edge of an ENT city. Remember your quest my friends. Keep close. Do not leave the paths for any reason," said King Arthur, "I will return to you at my palace."

They were just beginning. They would soon learn the pain of war.

Part 3

The war of the third earth has begun again, only this time no trolls or giants are left. The end might be farther away than expected.

Let me tell you about last time. There is an ancient rhyme that says: "One pyramid for six elves and dwarves feasting in their halls. One for sixteen riders of the night, one for the dark master in his hall of doom in the dark world where hate is power, one to find them all, one to hate them without reason, one to destroy them in the dark realm."

Merlin was in a fortress held by goblins. Rescuing him required a siege of the fort. Merlin called upon a soldier, black as a starless sky.

King Arthur was captured by goblins. He called on a warrior with a helm and a suit of armor of pure gold. His name was Uther Pendragon! They defeated the stupid orcs. They expelled the orcs from third earth forever, and replaced them with masses and masses of random kittens. The group had had enough with orcs. They captured the final pyramid! They were transported back home to the end of time.

*Bashville is a hobbit village. It has a butcher, a baker, a woodworker, and everybody knows you. It is busy around Christmas because they all want the best Yule log and fruitcake. Hobbit fruitcakes are made in Bashville, the hobbit capital.

The Dragon

Michael Sproat

Far away in an ancient land not of this earth, there lived four protectors who protected the sacred city. These four protected it from a dragon of shadows and its army. Using their elemental powers, eventually they tossed it into a time warp hoping it would never return. After that the four protectors, along with the city, celebrated the triumph over the dragon. Then the four protectors split up, each going back to his native lands. The Protector of Fire decided to stay in the city in case the dragon returned. So there he is still keeping watch in stone. Now only a myth. (If you can read this, you don't need glasses.)

Not even a hundred years had passed before the dragon was back. In its claws it held a stone, almost transparent. When the protectors tried to stop the dragon, it lifted up the stone. Then the stone broke apart, hitting each protector. They tried another assault only to find the stone had drained their powers. The dragon then scattered the stones hiding them in many land. The dragon defeated the protectors and ruled for over 10,000 years. The protectors by then could not do anything about it, so the dragon took them over and made them part of its dark army. (If you can still read this, you still don't need glasses.)

Finally five people arrived to triumph against the dragon: Ray with fire, Olivia with water, Jacob with electricity, J.P. with earth, and a protector with a new power, Avery with wind. At first the protectors were spread out, but then the dragon decided to destroy the cities and move everyone to a concentration camp. The protectors met and ran to the mountains. (Hi, it's me again. Guess what? You still don't need glasses.)

Then they set out on a quest which was to search for the sacred tower that was almost as sacred as the sacred city, but still not as sacred. That was still more sacred than the sacred rock and the sacred light bulb that doesn't do anything but sit there and sometimes falls, crushing innocent victims… Then some stuff happened that really wasn't all that important. At last they found the sacred tower and outside of it was a strange creature. The protectors got closer and closer to the monkey-like creature. They startled it and it started coughing "wolum, wolum." They decided to call it Peigel and moved on. When they went into the tower, some more stuff happened. When they got out, they got a giant rock and crushed the dragon with it. Then they had a big feast, but nobody came because this had happened so many times no one really cared. Moo, bah, cluck, BAGEL. Er, I mean the end. Yeah, sure, let's go with that. There is more, but nobody cared about it enough to write it down. Hello I back. Here's Johnny… or Phillip… or who ever I am. All this tonight on

"Sixty Minutes." The one doughnut to rule them all. Or none. The Panthers win the Super Bowl. This truly is the twilight zone. I know one thing about you. You are reading this.

The Dragon: Part 2
The Comedy Strikes Back

Yes, this is a continuation of "The Dragon." Why I wrote this one or the last one I don't know. It's probably because I have nothing better to do. So here we go.

Once the feast was over the tower disappeared. The evil being that was the master of the dragon came. The protectors tried their best but fell easily to the shadow demon. They realized that the only way to defeat this demon was with the Sword of Aknorah, a warrior who had saved the city countless times and was the source of the protector's power.

They found Peigel and he was obviously insane because on the way to Gourdor he said, "Luke I am your author."

They went to Gourdor to destroy the sacred, but still slightly evil, shoe that was connected to the sacred, but slightly evil gerbil. So people started giving the protectors money for some reason. It might have to do with the sign they were holding that said, "Give us money." However, I really don't think so. Eventually they came across a ring that gave people every power there is. It was dirty, so they sold it for two dollars. They ditched Peigel because he was cramping their style. So, like the dragon, they hit it with a big rock and ran away.

So later they decided to get the ring back. After they did that, they gave it to a monkey. Once they figured out where the Aknorah's tomb was, they went there. They went deep into the tomb where people never have gone. They got the Sword of Aknorah and left. On their journey they heard of the Cave of No Return and the Banana of Invincibility. They went in search of the cave, got the banana and never returned.

This stuff just pops into my head. WHAT NOW? WHAT NOW? WWHHHHHAAATT NNNOOOOOWWWWW.? THE ONE RING THE ONE RING TO THROW AT PEOPLE… Sorry about that. Now back to the story.

Once they got back to the village it was in ruins. There was no sign of anyone or the demon; there was no evidence of a struggle. They eventually noticed a portal in the sky and after a few seconds, the demon came out. They drew each fragment of the sword that was in the tomb. And after a long battle they just decided to hit it with the rock.

This is in honor of my rock Phillip. And my other rock named Average Joe.

Fairy Moon

Sarah Matlock

This moon I stare at, stares back at me, calls my name, tells me to come and sit. I sit. I see its outline, like a shimmering dust oozing from a solid crescent shape, reminding me of dew on a fairy, a shimmering, wet look. So tempting, to just fly and swim with the comets.

The shimmer fades into a purple haze drifting across the moon, blocking the shimmer. The faint outline of a crescent is still here. And the faint outlines of stars around it… But are they stars? They look like fairies, dancing with the moon. I watch as the haze fades. The shimmer appears; fairies turn back into their star shape. Am I imagining? Are they like gargoyles appearing only in a purple haze? They dance when it seems no one is near. I myself have found out their secret. I shall keep this a secret. I will tell it to my granddaughters when they are born. We shall sit when the moon whispers; we shall sit, and watch the fairies dance.

Humor

Avery Brakebill
Winton Burst
Josh DiGiovanni
Granger Endsley
Daniel Lawrence
Evan Lohrey

The Trouble with Dragons

Avery Brakebill

OOPS. I really didn't mean to pull that switch with all the laser traps around it. Honestly I didn't, it just worked out that way. But that was four years ago. Oh well now there are dragons around every corner. Now this old geezer wants me to go flip that switch *again*. Be right back, an old blue dragon is on his way. By the way, I'm Avange.

Where was that tower? Where's my map? Oh well, I think I can remember where the tower of Harasyamo is.

"Ouch!"

So that's where my dagger was! Oh well. Time to go to the town market. Let's see how much money I have. $50!!!!! I'm richer than I thought.

"Yeah, hi I'd like to buy that pig, cow, and that Cornish-game hen," said I.

"How you gonna pay for dat?" he pondered.

"With this."

"Whoa! Where'd you get that?"

"Work. So what if I have a job?"

After that I left the market place and met up with my friends and a gold dragon.

"Hey man, time for the meeting," one of them reminded me.

I went to the meeting where we decided who would go with me to flip the switch. Well it's decided. Michael, Mikhail, and I will go to the tower to flip that switch. Thank the lord that that is decided.

"Whoa what is going on?"

Why are we all glowing? Whoa we have super natural powers.

I can make the wind and the waters bend to my will.

"MWAHAHA!"

"Who said that?" Out come the swords, fire balls, lasers, staffs, and daggers.

All of a sudden I say, "Hooshemakamaka, hooshemakamaka." So that's how you get the shield to work. What? It's not like it came with an operating manual.

After that we met up with a girl named Olivia, a guy named Jacob, and a guy named JP. Then we went and got attacked by a gigantic evil Dragon of Shadows. We fought for twenty-two hours and we got wounded and Mikhail got killed. After that Michael changed his name to Ray. Then I used a vengeance spell and we beat the daylights out of that dragon, only to find out that it was a machine. Then we met up with little lizard men called nuets. We took them prisoner and made them lead the way to the CAVE OF WUTDAHAYISIT.

When we got there we found out that there were two people named Ray. So we fought to see which was real and Michael/Ray won, so we killed the other guy. BOOM! BOOM! BOOM! BOOM! BOOM! BOOM! Uh-oh, here comes a giant to add to the list of troubles. Oh great it's hungry.

"Hooshemakamaka, hooshemakamaka," I said.

Up goes the shield. Well good thing I bought the hen, the pig, and the cow. So we bought our lives with the animals and the giant thanked us by taking us to the tower.

Now is where the dragons come into this story. Wait. Why are there little munchkins singing "Follow the Yellow Brick Road?"

"You guys are in the wrong story," I said.

"We are? Sorry," they said.

Now that that's over with up the tower we go. There's the switch, but what happened to the lasers? OH that's what. A dragon ate 'em. Now we gotta go and kill this dragon. Then my sword felt hot so I accidentally threw it at the dragon that was the emperor's. So I flipped the switch and the evil dragons turned to dust.

BEEP.

BEEP.

BEEP.

Whoa! What a dream!

Evan Lohrey

Hi! I Am Pavilion

Evan Lohrey

Hi, I am Pavilion. My mom was named Hewlett. My dad was named Packard. I am a middle school laptop, one of the very worst jobs a laptop can have. Just imagine being owned by somebody who does not know how to take care of you, throwing you around, dropping you, and the worst of all, being mean to you.

Luckily, my first owner was a sweet kid, somebody who knew how to treat me. In case you don't know, I was employed at Greenway school. I was a newcomer just like my owner. He was in sixth grade and getting used to Greenway just as I was. My owner loved to play my games. They were the best since they came in my programming and they were 3D.

The school year went by and summer began. At first I was weary of this time, since I would not be turned on in a long time. But as the days passed I got used to it. One good experience I got out of it was that I got to talk and socialize with the other laptops. The older laptops passed on their wisdom, while my fellow new laptops got to see who was the best. In the end it was kinda like a camp.

The next year was pretty much like the last, except I had to go and get fixed. It was not a big problem though, because a small part of me needed to be replaced or repaired. I don't know which since they put me to sleep first. Well, it was a success and my owner got me back as good as new.

My owner's last year at Greenway was the worst one yet. I knew that he would be leaving, but I did not know if I would be going with him.

The days were progressing and getting shorter and shorter. It was getting colder and colder outside. We were getting closer to that one time when everybody was happy. It was finally Christmas and everybody had left for the break. The laptops all celebrated their own little holidays. Some celebrated Hanukkah and others celebrated Christmas. I personally celebrated Christmas since my owner celebrated it, but I did not have anything to give or get. I did make the best out of it, though. Instead of a tree, I had a screen; instead of lights, I had bytes; instead of Saint Nick, I had Rick (the repairman); instead of gifts, I had gigs; and finally instead of family, I got memory. Well my laptop friends thought I was crazy, but I knew what it actually was. They were jealous. I was having fun on a holiday and they weren't. Even though I had every thing, I still was lonely.

When my owner came back from break, I was so happy to see him. As the weeks passed we got closer and closer to the end of the school year. Also, the days got longer and longer and warmer and warmer. I was now being called an old laptop by the younger laptops, since I was with a eighth grader and I had been there for three years. My comeback was not as clever as the new laptops' comebacks (They had bigger processors), but it was "So if I am so old, why do I know more than you. Oh that's right, I have had the chance to gain it."

It was ten days before the end of the year and from my owner's actions, I could tell that he was not as interested in me as he used to be. I was so afraid that if he didn't buy me, I would get the most horrible of students next year. Also if I was to get a kid as good as he was, I would still miss him. It would be hard not to miss a kid when you have been with him for practically your whole life. It was almost time for the end of the year. He was happy, yet a little sad. I think he was happy because it was finally summer, but he also knew that he probably would not get to see his friends from school in a long time, if ever. But what was bothering me was not knowing if he was going to buy me.

It was the last week and I did not expect that he had bought me. I was pretty sad during that week. Most of the laptops were so happy since their owners were pretty abusive. On the last day there was so many celebrations and the students were having fun, a lot of fun. When the graduation ceremony was over and the food ceremony was starting, there was a lot of remembering. Finally, the eighth graders and my owner were ready to go. They started to leave and my owner had actually gone out the door and was what I thought leaving, when he came back in and said that he had forgotten something. He was coming over to me and he picked me up and left with me. I was so happy, he had actually taken me with him.

This is when the tale of my past ends and the story of my future begins. I have actually been with him for five years now (including Greenway). I have actually gotten a strange message from my old laptop friends from Greenway that the abused laptops have bad owners again. That's not all of it though. They are so fed up that they are organizing a revolt, A GRAND REVOLT, not just being bad. They are not going to be secretive anymore. They are going to attack their owners and even the other students. So don't go to Greenway for a while (It won't look pretty.). Bye.

Just Because

Granger Endsley

"*You* killed him!" yelled Luke desperately.

And then you hear Darth Vader say menacingly, "No, Luke, you don't understand. I am your aunt's college roommate's fourth cousin's nephew three times removed…wait…or am I your old Boy Scout leader's son to the third power squared…no. But I'm not your father and you know it. The point is we're related."

I was just thinking, what *if* Darth Vader had said that…Oh, well.

The two paragraphs you've just read have absolutely NOTHING to do with this story at all. This story has no real plot, setting, or characters. But it *does* have a meaning. And that meaning is simply to entertain you and make you think about things. I already have, haven't I?

I've heard that people have more dreams about snakes than any other animal. I find that hard to believe. I have never once in my life (that I can remember, of course) had a dream about snakes.

When my sister tells me about her dreams, I can only wonder what they actually look like.

For instance, whenever we go to *Ryan's*, I almost always get a cookie for dessert. Every time this happens, she says, "It's the cookie from the stairs!" Nowadays, I just grin because I know exactly what she means. Whereas, the first time it happened, well, I can't remember exactly what I did or said…but oh well. You probably want to hear all about the dream now, correct? I thought so.

When you're reading this keep in mind that my sister was about six years old when she had this dream. OK, this is how the dream started: She and I were trick-or-treating without anybody else with us. Now, in a dream, you don't take the time to think about things like this. If this dream were real, then we probably would've been panicking (Since I was about nine and she was about six). The point is that in a dream, you don't have to worry about things such as being alone on Halloween night because you know that everything is going to turn out OK in the end. I'm getting off the topic here, aren't I? Sorry about that.

As I was saying, in this dream we were trick-or-treating all by ourselves when we came to a specific house. We walked right up to it and knocked on the door. When the door opened, we saw a little old lady standing there who immediately said, "Oh, come in."

Now, once again I am going to go into the thing about how incredibly unintelligent people can be in dreams, because what do you think we did? We walked right in, of course.

Wow, now that I look back at what I've written, I can imagine what you might be thinking: "How can this possibly tie in to getting dessert at Ryan's?" Well you're about to find out.

As we walked inside, the old woman led us into her house and after about six feet or so she led us around a U-turn to the left and down some stairs. On the third step--listen closely--there was a cookie just sitting there with three chocolate chips. If you put a triangle inside a circle, and say the circle is the cookie, the three chocolate chips will be where the points of the triangle are.

When the old lady saw us both eyeing the cookie, she said, "Help yourselves." We both dived for it and accidentally broke it in two.

After we had eaten it, the old lady said to us, "I'll give you a choice. You can stay here with me forever, and have all the cookies you want, or you can go back home."

I'm going to give you one guess as to what our answer was. If you guessed that we were stupid enough to choose the first choice, you were right! And before you start thinking this is just another Hansel-

and-Gretel story, well, the dream actually just ends right there.

So in conclusion, not only people can be incredibly unintelligent in dreams, but also thing like the way a dream ends doesn't make any sense...What shall we talk about next?

The Chicken or the Egg

Daniel Lawrence

Hi. I'm the Chicken. I used to live on a big smelly farm, but I got bored and decided to move out. After 8 days of solid hitchhiking and Super 8 motels, I finally reached my destination, New York City. Mind you, I had no money, so actually staying IN a motel was impossible; however, the dumpster was always free and cozy. Hey, I'm a Chicken! You think I care about hygiene?

Well NY seemed pretty nice. There were many people. Half of them seemed to have a need to grab their ear and talk to a little box, as if it was listening. HA! These people are hilarious! Everything seemed to be going fine with my life. I was walking down the road, seeking employment, (I'm too short to wave a taxi), when I saw a large KFC with a "Help Wanted" sign in the window. I thought, "This is perfect for me! I can be the spokesman!" I walked inside to seek the manager, and upon meeting him, proceeded to tell him my qualifications. I really couldn't tell if he was listening. He just seemed to stare at me in a strange, longing way. After I finished my employment speech, he stood up. He was a tall, skinny man. He told me that he might have a "Job" for me in the kitchen. I started to get worried so I ran away, very quickly.

It was getting dark when I reached a kind of bad district. It was there that I found the next chapter of my life, as a taxi driver. I was walking past the Yellow Taxi station. For some reason it was really loud inside. It sounded like two people arguing. I just stood, listening, until finally one person stormed out of the building, and another person put a Help Wanted sign in the window. It was my chance! I decided that I should be a taxi driver right then, so rushed inside to meet my fate.

It turns out that a short, fat, greasy man named Chuck monitored my fate. Here's how it went. I walked inside and promptly met up with the man who had put the Help Wanted sign in the window. I asked him where I could apply for a job, and he showed me Chuck's office. That place was so full of smoke, mold, and grime that I could hardly cough out my education. It was not really like it mattered. After I had finished my application speech, I asked if I could have the job. No answer. I asked again. No answer. I got off my chair and walked around the smoke-smothered desk to find Chuck sleeping peacefully. I woke him up, and he asked me some questions. Did I have a driver's license? "No! But did any taxi drivers have one?" Was I old enough? "Of course," and, finally, he asked me if I was willing to have a car without cruise control. I had to think about this one. I mean I'm going to have to have my foot to that pedal all day. Then again? Is it even possible to use cruise control in New York? So off I wen to meet my car. Well…it was a bit big for me, but it was a living.

One day, I was cruising around town, and was flagged down by two philosophers. You know…it was quite odd really… they didn't want a ride, but rather had flagged me down because I was a Chicken. Apparently they had spent the past 7 years arguing about whether the Chicken or the Egg came first, and so far had not found either the right answer or a chicken to answer it for them. I pondered this for a while, and finally decided that I really didn't know. The men gave me their phone number and asked me to call them if I thought of the answer. Then they were off, arguing about what to get for lunch.

That evening, I sat on my couch in my apartment, watching *Oprah*, when my mind wandered to that fateful question. Which DID come first? I really didn't know. I thought of Mom, back at home in New Jersey. She would probably know the answer. Mom always seemed to know everything. After about thirty minutes of thinking about my family, I decided that it was time to return home. I had seen the outside world, and it just was not fitting me.

The next day I quit my job as the taxi driver. That was easy, seeing as how Chuck the manager was asleep again when I resigned.

How was I to get back home? I had hardly any money and no means of private transportation. I eventually decided that I should take a bus. It was faster and more comfortable than hitchhiking, plus there was a bathroom in the back.

When it was time to go, I grabbed a newspaper and boarded the bus. It was a kind of old bus. There were soup stains on the carpet and gum under my seat. The whole thing creaked, but it was a mode of transportation. Oh and remember that bathroom I told you about? It was out of order. VERY out of order. Halfway home the bus broke down.

We were stuck on the side of the highway for three hours until a replacement bus could come.

What seemed like days later, I finally arrived home. It looked mostly the same, except for a new silo. I regretted returning to my home at first. All the dangers, you know. Getting fat and then eaten, etc. When I had been back there for a while, I was really happy that I returned.

So that's my story. I'm tired. I think I'm going to go up to bed. It's been a rough day. I hope you've enjoyed my story! Oh, and...Don't listen to what those Chick-Fil-A Cows have to say. It's not true! EAT MORE COWS!

PS. The egg came first.

The Thanksgiving Feud

Winton Burst

I am "the famous one" when Thanksgiving rolls around. And no one even knows my name, probably because I cannot talk. That is no big deal because I can write. I know that if I get the word out to people that chicken is a better choice for Thanksgiving, people will feast upon *them* every year. So I need all the students to help me with my cause. It is really a shame that every time I go out on Thanksgiving an evil little brat tries to gun me down with a BB gun.

But this time they will pay! My friends and I have gathered paintball guns from all over the city to start "The Rebellion of the Turkeys." We have the finest assortment of paintball guns you could ever think of. Tomorrow is the date of the big war. The declaration of war is being prepared as we speak (or write). In about three hours it will strike twelve o'clock and the Invasion of Thanksgiving will begin.

It is now time to start the advance and I am pumped and ready to go to war. At least I think I am.

Uh oh. We have incoming!

Get down.

Clank, clank, clank. Thud, thud, thud. Three turkeys hit the ground in a burst of paint. We were next.

And so the great saga of the Thanksgiving Feud was over before the turkeys could even get out of their cave to start attacking. It ended up that the great power of paintball guns left no turkeys untouched or unpainted. Red and green paint was splattered everywhere.

Oh well. They won't be expecting us at Christmas.

Youth Soccer

Josh DiGiovanni

Youth soccer is teaching basic skill, respect for rules and good sportsmanship, but what is actually learned in those twelve weeks? As a coach you learn a lot. For example, you learn it's too cold to play without a blanket when it's forty degrees outside. Or, my personal favorite "My mom wants me to wear a poncho so I don't get sick." You never stop hearing, "Can we go yet? Is this thing over?"

Practice is grueling, never knowing where all the players are, finding them sitting on their parent's laps or on the playground. As one of the coaches, you need to realize that they want to play around and that you need to make practice fun for them.

"It is better than video games or TV," I explain.

"No it is not. Video games are cooler," shriek the players.

I explain, "Soccer is a great sport. Give it a chance."

As a coach, you also have to focus on getting ready for a game with drills.

The coach announces, "Let's do some sprints."

"I'm tired. Can we go?" whines a little girl.

Another player asks, "Is it a race? I like races."

I yell, "Yes, it's like a race. Go!"

After practice, I have a team talk. "Tomorrow is our first game. Be here at 8:15 to warm up."

I tell them 8:15 so there will be a chance of having enough players by game time. They gradually show up, saying "My mom overslept." Or "I couldn't find my jersey."

I say, "All right it's time for the line up. Who wants to be in the goal, a goalkeeper? How about you, Tim?"

Tim moans, "Can I sit out this quarter and next quarter?"

I say, "Go play keeper!"

"Do you mean goalie?"

"No, Tim, soccer is a keeper; hockey is a goalie."

"Who brought snacks, coach?" another kid asks.

I reply, "Don't worry about that now."

I finally read the line up and we are ready to play. I pump them up, saying "Hands in. One, two, three…go Warriors." Picking the team name…that was the favorite practice so far.

The captains come back to the sideline. I ask, "Who is kicking off and which way?"

"I think that way and we are kicking off."

Again I try to pump them up. "Are you guys ready? Let's go score a goal!"

The whistle sounds; the game begins. We have the ball. They do the kick off the way we practiced. They are actually passing. A miracle... Maybe they just need some competitive atmosphere.

We win our first game, but would only win one more the rest of the season. The players could care less.

It is finally the last practice. There will be a parent and coaches against the kids game. We will also do their favorite game, Butts Up against the Coaches. This is a game where the coaches bend down in the goal and the players try to hit the coaches in the butt with a shot using their feet, not their hands.

Now, it is time for the last game. The players are excited, ready to go...to the end of the year party. We win the game, but not before I hear "Can I sit out? I don't like that position." But we win 4-3.

Now it is time for the highlight of the year. It is party time. That means one thing to the players: pizza, cake and their trophies. The head coach hands out the trophies and thanks the assistants. Then we watch a DVD that one of the parents made about the season, with highlights and music. It is over and it is time to say goodbye. The players could care less because most of them go to school together.

It is over. Time to get back to a regular Saturday for me. My soccer season has started. We start traveling and soon I will not have to yell, "Get up!" or look for straying players. You would think that I wouldn't miss it, but I do. I start to realize that maybe I taught these kids something. Maybe they will take something away from this experience.

Life

Demetrius Green
Brianna Kirby
Amber Lovett
Clancy Oliver
Lili Sarayrah
Mollie Uphoff
Forrest Wentzel

All Alone on Christmas Eve

Mollie Uphoff

I can hear birds singing in the trees.
I can feel the cold ice water
Running down my face
As my tears turn to ice.
I use to love Christmas.
Now, I am all alone
And have nowhere to go.
I am all alone on Christmas Eve.
No family
No church
No friends
I am all alone and I am here

Under a tree with icicles falling on
me
As I cry.
I can hear caroling.
I can smell the hot cocoa the carolers
bring.
I can see their footprints in the snow.
I can try to walk home,
But I just can't find the guts to do
this.
This is something I can do,
But don't.
Christmas is all about family
But I can't spend another moment
With my family
Ever, ever again.

Being a Twin

Clancy Oliver

What is it like to be a twin? Well, you may not have experienced it before, but I always will. I'll tell you one thing. It's a bad experience for the parents. But another thing is it can be worse from the twin's point of view. Usually it's great to have two girls, and then it's good to have two boys, but it's usually bad to have one boy and one girl. Well, I have a twin sister and my twin sister has a twin brother so, yes, my parents had a boy and a girl.

My name is Clancy and I am the boy. I'm a perfectionist and I'm creative and very curious. I always have liked to build things. I like playing with my kitten and my favorite subject is math. I'm 12 years old and my birthday is August 3. My favorite holiday is Christmas and my favorite color is orange. I live in Knoxville, TN and I have a big brother whose name is Sam.

My twin sister is the girl and she is almost completely the opposite of me. She is creative too, but in a different way. She is the opposite of a perfectionist and she isn't that curious. Her favorite color isn't mine and her favorite subject is NO subject. She complains quite a bit. She didn't really ever like building things either. I think that just about the only similarities that my twin and I have are that we both have the same relatives, we're both humans, and we both have the same birthday and are the same age and are in the same grade.

My experience was pretty fun when I was a toddler or a young kid, but it's just gone downhill from there. Hopefully when I grow up, it will be better once again. There are small problems like stealing candy and causing tardy slips, but then there are big things like being puked on or getting gum stuck in your hair.

A lot of things have happened to me and to my twin, but we survived, mainly thanks to my parents, but it still remains pretty bad. My twin and I don't kill each other, but we do fight a lot. We both feel sorry for each other, but that happens rarely. I usually don't like having a twin sister. It's not always that bad, but I still hate that terrible word, twin.

How Nothing Became Something

Forrest Wentzel

Once upon a time there was a guy with the name of Nothing. People didn't know much about Nothing or what was going on up there in his head. Nothing was the most bored person on earth. You can look it up in the Guinness World Record book. He just sat around and did, as his name suggests, nothing. Sometimes he thought about things, but only about how bored he was.

One day he was actually thinking and something came to his mind. What if he actually tried to do something? Nah, forget it, it was too crazy. It was so crazy it just might work. He did so much thinking that he couldn't stand it any more and he passed out.

Sure, Nothing was always bored, but deep down in his heart he was proud of being so bored. He didn't know he was in any books, but he was told by the people who came to his house that he was special. Very special.

One day Nothing remembered his idea of doing something. He thought he might try. First, he thought he might try to open his eyes. He tried and tried and tried. He got one eyelid to slowly open and then the other and … "AAARRRRGGHH," he yelled. He made a lot of progress that day. He opened his eyes and learned to make noises such as "YAHNGNGNG," AND "PAGAGAGAGAG," AND "GOOOGOOOGOOO," AND "HARGATRAOOOOOO." He was almost like a caveman except he wasn't moving or using tools.

The next day he was so tired from all the work he did the day before. He did amuse himself by making noises and groaning. Later that day, his mother, who visited him every once in a while, came to see him. She was a very pretty woman and a very nice woman. She wore simple clothes and was not extremely skinny and not overweight at all. As soon as she walked in, Nothing said, "HOOGLADOOOLUMP."

His mother was amazed about how he had his eyes open and how he was making noises. She walked over to him and patted him on the back.

In a sweet voice, she said, "I am your mommy. I love you and will always take care of you." Then she left and Nothing was alone again.

Later that day, his father came in. He was a big man, not fat, but big and had big muscles. He was the kind of person who if you ran into him on the street you would run away. Despite his appearance, he was about the nicest person you would ever meet. The second he walked in the door, Nothing shouted, "MOMMA."

His father chuckled and said, "No, Nothing, I'm not your mother. I am your dad."

Nothing was confused and asked, "Huh?"

His father had by now decided that his son wanted to become more like a normal person. He held out his hand and saw that Nothing tried to reach out and grab it. Nothing tried his hardest and finally grabbed his dad's caring hand.

Then his dad reached out for Nothing's other hand and the same thing happened. His dad tried to help him stand up and Nothing also tried to stand up. With their joined effort, Nothing stood up for the first time. Suddenly his knees buckled and he fell over and hit his head and every thing went black.

His father immediately called an ambulance to get him. Then Nothing heard the loud, obnoxious sound of the siren rushing towards his house. They rushed Nothing to the hospital.

The next thing Nothing saw was a doctor sticking a lollipop in his face. Nothing grabbed it with his mouth and sucked on it, with a huge smile. The doctor told Nothing's dad that he would be just fine. Poor Nothing had no idea what was going on. He could barely think, let alone move around well. While they were at the hospital, they had Nothing fitted for leg braces to help him stand and move a little bit. They also got a wheel chair for Nothing.

They began walking out of the hospital. As they reached the exit door, Nothing's father began coughing. He felt a sharp pain in his chest. He fell to the ground and that was the last thing that Nothing's father ever did.

Nothing nudged him with his wheel chair, but he didn't move. He tried again and failed. It was then that Nothing realized that something bad had happened.

He yelled, "UH OH!!!"

The hospital workers ran over to his dad, put him on a stretcher and rushed him into the emergency room. They checked for a heart rate and there wasn't one. The doctor walked to Nothing, who was sitting in a corner.

"Nothing," the doctor said quietly, "your dad is no longer with us."

Nothing may not have been too smart, but he was smart enough to realize that his dad was dead. Slowly, Nothing began crying. He started with one tear that grew and grew until it was a roaring sob, sobbing like a mother who had lost her child. This was a sight enough to make any grown man cry.

Everyone in that emergency room tried to comfort Nothing, but they could not do it without crying with him. The doctor, of all people, who had seen many people die, was crying the most of all of them. That goes to show just how moving this scene was.

Nothing, for a long time, was just a lump that didn't move or do anything. What he did do may not seem like a lot, but when you think about what he was like before, he was like he was not even alive. Now he was actually something. Now, he could make a difference in the world.

Students often say “I have nothing to write about.” I reply “Then, write about nothing.” That is the origin of this story.

Magic Johnson: Athlete Gone Biz

Demetrius Green

Magic Johnson is widely known for his 12 years in the NBA, but is rarely recognized for his many contributions to the advancement of African-American neighborhoods. His accomplishments include starting many theatres in the black community, starting a line of T.G.I Fridays and Starbucks, and also promoting the awareness of the HIV virus.

One of the things Magic Johnson did in the neighborhoods was start business. Some of his businesses include restaurants, coffee shops, and expanding urban ownerships. One of the greatest accomplishes that he is known for would probably be his addition of theatres in urban areas. He put these mega theatres in underprivileged locations where movie theatres of such humungous sizes are not usually found. This was done with a partnership with Sony Entertainment motion pictures exhibition group. These theaters have seating ranging from fitting 3,200 to 5,000 people. A few reasons they were made were to help promote economical growth, job development, and financial power. Another object of this mission was to operate first-rate multiplex theatres in black communities. Johnson wanted his theatres to be filled with comfort, style, and care. Another big thing he put into his theatre designs was advanced technology. An example of the high technology is computerized box office stations, gorgeously designed lobbies with many concession stands, stadium size seating, and state of the art SDSS stereo sound. In addition to providing an excellent theatrical entertainment experience, the theatre offer business stimulus, fostering local economical growth, job development, and financial empowerment to the communities they serve.

Another one of the things Magic Johnson did was make his own line of T.G.I. Friday restaurants. This was done with a partnership with Carlson Restaurants. Carlson Restaurants is based in Dallas, Texas, and is considered an important innovator in the fight to bring in jobs, vitality, entertainment, and casual dining options to black development of both casual and sophisticated dining segments. The restaurants were communities. Magic Johnson also made a partnership with Starbucks. Together, they try to enthusiastically satisfy customers while contributing to the community development and the environment. The jointly owned shops are a social center in the communities. Magic Johnson really helped the black community to me by making a bunch of jobs for black people.

Another thing Johnson did was make black people more aware that HIV virus is real and is out there so they should go get tested. He did many events to make people a lot more aware of HIV, especially black people. That is very important because before then HIV was like the dark ages, everyone knew what it was but no one thought it would happen to them, sort of like how a teenager might feel when he's driving a car- invincible. Magic Johnson was like a light, showing people the truth about HIV. It's really there and it could happen to anybody. He donated thousands to HIV awareness groups. He wants people to know the effects that having AIDS will have on them. Everyone should be prepared, so he's helping them.

That is why I think Johnson is the greatest millionaire. He got sick, had to retire, but he still over came all of that and is helping everyone else be more aware. He also put more businesses in the black community, giving them more jobs. Which makes him, to me, the black American millionaire who made the most significant contributions to the advancements of blacks in America.

My Experience in Middle School

Brianna Kirby

I go to middle school.
Hmmm…what can I say?
I always get into trouble,
But it's not my fault…no way!
I try to stay out of trouble
And I try to have good days,
But as soon as I touch someone,
The teacher yells "PDA!"
I really think something is wrong
with me.
It's hard to follow these rules.

I mean, every time I talk in class,
I'm sent out of the modules!
And when I try to ask questions
They tell me to be quiet.
They tell me my voice carries,
And I'm going to start a riot.
They make me sit all by myself,
That makes me feel like an outcast.
I argue and argue and finally obey,
But they just don't understand…I
might not last.
You see, I'm a social bug,
I just can't help it!
I'm just a happy kid,
I mean literally ecstatic!
So that's middle school
And don't get me wrong,
It's a pretty good school,
But it's lasting too long.
I just wish...O, I wish
The teachers would get off my back!
They know I can't help it,
They should cut me some SLACK!

Love,

Lili Sarayrah

2005

The Dreaded Journey

Lili Sarayrah

I wake to the clatter and clang of breakfast dishes. I bet it will be ready soon. I stretch, sit up and look around at my beloved room. There's Nelly, on the floor. I smile and pick her up. Rolling out of bed, I step to the window to see the weather. A beautiful day! But then, I remember. Today is the day my adventure starts.

Someone patters up the stairs, and soon I hear a soft rap on the door. Mama's voice says, "We have ham and eggs this morning, come down quick!"

I mumble something like "coming." Maybe I shouldn't get out of bed at all.

"Mama, I'm sick!" I yell, but she's already out of earshot.

I put on a sweater and throw open the door. The smell of ham is wafting up the stairwell and fills me with longing for the familiar dining table we always eat at. I will sorely miss it.

"Mama, I'm scared," I whisper, a little out of breath.

"Oh, no!" exclaims Mama, "Don't worry. I left the pepper out of your eggs."

I harrumph and sit down at the table. It's not pepper I'm worried about.

"Do you want me to help?"

Anything to take my mind off my looming departure!

"No, I'm fine."

She's probably worried I'll drop a dish or something.

"Mama, I need to ask you a question."

"Hmmm?"

"What would you say if I went traveling soon?"

"Why, that's entirely your decision!" laughed Mama, "You're a roaming bird. I can see that."

She must be joking. Right? Would she really let me go?

Maybe I haven't spent enough time with her lately. Even so, I'm just a little hurt.

"All right. I'll leave right after breakfast."

"Where will you go?"

"Wherever the wind takes me," I mumble and stuff a piece of toast down my throat to avoid further awkward conversation.

"All right," Mama sighed, "I never can seem to keep steady customers."

I turn around too fast to see her impish smile and think she's serious. I'll miss her sweet nature, almost as much as Lily's piping voice. But I think it's time to see more of the world.

Mama turns on the hot water and starts washing the dishes. She's constantly busy, always doing something constructive. That's why she can single-handedly run the boarding house. I know she doesn't have much money to spread around, so I'm not expecting any to help me get going and out of the house. Well, maybe a little for lunch.

With no other excuse to stay at the table I clear my plate and go back up the stairs slowly, looking at the family portraits that line the walls.

My room is going to be a definite loss. I'm so used to its shapes and shadows! Maybe I'll just go away for a little while. That sounds good. But, what should I take? Won't everything be lonely?

This is frightening. I grab wildly and pack everything I can. I feel like I want to pack my room up in a box! Now I'm bouncing up and down on my bag, trying to get it shut. Bounce, bounce, bounce CRACK! This won't work. I'll have to leave something. Then I'll have something nice to come back to. Now I slowly start to unpack my bag and repack with only my essentials. This all fits. Good. Now I should go, before I change my mind.

"Ma, I'm ready to go," I call, my voice dangerously close to cracking.

"All right. Do you need anything?" she inquires.

"No. I'll be fine."

"Okay, see you later. Have fun!" Mama smiles warmly at me.

Oh, Nelly! I forgot! I fetch the floppy rag doll, pull open the door and go. It's a gorgeous day in the fall, just warm enough. I sit down on the swing in the front yard, dragging my bag and Nelly, and watch the big yellow school bus that will take me on my journey to first grade as it comes rumbling down the street.

The Story of a Boy

Amber Lovett

"Luke, I am your…mother!" I am Luke and that's my mother. I hear that too much.

"Now, Luke, what did you think you were doing when you went to the movies without telling me?" my mother asks.

Here is what is going on. I went to the movies with a couple of friends. The movie was over and I went to call my mom and tell her where I was because I hadn't told her before, but I forgot. Then, when I got home, she was standing there in the doorway waiting for an explanation. Here is how it went.

"Umm, well, I was going to tell you when…We were…uh I…I…" I stammer.

"You know if you go any where you must tell me where you are going!" my mother says, screaming at this point.

"MOM! Please don't yell at me! This is ridiculous. I was going to call you after the movie was over and tell you when I was going to get home,' I say, trying to explain in a calm way to my overprotective mother.

"I am very disappointed in you, so I will have to ground you. Now, go to your room and think about what you did and tell me a good reason why you did that."

"OK," I say while I am walking up the stairs.

When I get to my room, I think. *Maybe I didn't call because I didn't think you were at home, so I waited until the movie was over because I thought you were shopping and...Oh, wait, I have used that one before*

Well, I know a good reason. I didn't want to call because I was late for the movie anyway and I didn't know if you were home or not. OK, I will just mix these two fake reasons and she will buy it...hopefully.

"MOM!" I yell, to get her attention.

"What do you need Luke?"

"Come up here. I need to talk to you."

"OK, I am coming," my mom yells.

"Well, Mom, see this is what happened. See we were late for the movie and I thought you went to the store. So that is why I didn't call you." I try to remember what I was going to say.

"Well, I don't think I can believe that!" my mom says.

"OK. Then I was going to call you when I got outside, but it was too noisy, so I figured I probably couldn't hear you," I say, trying not to make it too obvious that I was making it up.

"Well, I still don't believe you," my mom says once more.

"OK…The real reason is I didn't want to call you so I wouldn't get into trouble for going to the movies without telling you…but…I guess…that didn't…really work," I reply cluelessly.

"Well, then, you guessed right! You are grounded again. You can't go out anywhere for two weeks."

"No Mom! Please! My church group is going to the Haunted Corn Maze on Sunday," I cry.

It's Sunday, the day of the corn maze. I have to convince my mom to let me go.

"MOM!" I yell.

"What is it? I am trying to cook dinner," she yells back.

"I'm ready to go to the corn maze. Can you take me? It starts in thirty minutes," I scream back.

I hear footsteps coming up the stairs and my door opens.

"Luke, I have considered this for a long time. I am sorry, but you can't go," my mother says calmly.

"Why can't I go?" I ask.

"You know what you did, and we won't argue about it," Mom says.

"OK. Fine. I'm going to bed early tonight. I'm tired."

My mom goes downstairs again and soon I hear stuff going on in the kitchen.

Hmm. How can I go to the corn maze when I don't have a ride and my mom will be in the living room right by the door? I know. I'll call a friend and sneak out of the window. I can get back at ten. Mom will be in bed and she'll never know about it.

I call Julia, hoping she isn't doing anything tonight.

"Hello," Julia answers.

"Hey, it's Luke. Are you doing anything tonight because I need a ride to the corn maze," I tell her.

"I'm not doing anything. What time do you want me to pick you up?" Julia asks.

"About 8:30," I reply.

"OK, I'll be there.

Good. I have a ride. Now to make a plan to get out of the house. Let's see. I can make a rope with my

sheets and do that thing where they climb out of the window. I can make a fake person in my bed to make it look like I am sleeping there. How do I do that?
I can use my basketball for my head and pillows for my body. I just hope she doesn't try to give me a kiss goodnight.

"Mom, I am going to bed now," I tell my mom while she is watching TV.

"OK, good night," she replies.

HONK. HONK. That must be Julia. I hope she doesn't bother Mom. I tie the rope and go down very slowly so I don't fall.

"Hey, Julia," I say with joy.

"Glad to help. So, why did you get grounded in the first place?" she asks.

"Oh, forgot to call Mom when I went out to the movies," I explained. "But enough of that. Turn left here. Keep going. I will need you to pick me up about 9:45," I tell her.

"No problem," she tells me.

I really enjoy the maze, but when 9:45 comes, no Julia. The maze owner makes me call my mom because they didn't want to get into trouble.

"Oh, no!" I scream. "SHE IS GOING TO KILL ME."

I am going to be so grounded. What can I do? I will have to hide or something. I am so dead.

When my mom arrives to pick me up, she doesn't look very happy.

"Hey, Mom, looks like it is you and me on the way home," I say, trying to cover up that I am worried.

Mom doesn't talk to me the whole way. Until we get home...!

"This is the same thing that happened three days ago with the movies. What is wrong with you?" she yells. "I am very worried about you. I think you will be grounded for another two weeks!" Mom says.

"OK, I will never do this again," I say.

I think I may need to stay home for a while.

Pondering

Olivia Burn
J.P. Campbell
Christian Hendrix
Brianna Hope
Julia Neely
Hannah Nodell
Miranda Uphoff
Nikki Winters

Shiny Silver

(a creative writing assignment on a Hershey's Kiss)

J.P. Campbell

Shiny silver
Kiss in blue

Flat bottom
Covered in foil

Smells sugary
Smells good

No sound
Doesn't bounce

Heavenly good
Great, awesome

My taste buds just went to heaven
With a side trip to paradise.

A Ballad of Thought

Olivia Burn

It seems like everyone is searching
for something,
but what?
We seek it,
but do we look in the wrong places?
Is religion the source,
the fountain that the truly righteous
can drink from
and understand all?
Or does it flow and drown everyone?

Many wonder if religion is the whole
truth,
or part of the truth?
If so, then which one?

Is religion what has people acting
and saying what they are not to each
other to be better accepted,

or to be destined for eternal pain?
The people of this group are told that
if they believe without a doubt,
there will be a reward of eternal
wonders that will reward the worthy
beyond what anyone can imagine.
Is this the truth?

Or is religion so vague in beliefs that
one must search within oneself to
find the truth, only reaching
enlightenment
on earth near the time of death,
but leaving most all others to find
enlightenment
only in the afterlife?
Is this the truth?

There are many others,
all of which have faults,
but which is right?
Should one be with the religion they
are guided to,
or search for one themselves?
Should someone who believes in the
"true" try to make others conform
and shun them at their refusal,
or let anyone come of their on
accord?

If you do not understand what all

people search for,
reflect on your life until you
understand.
If you've never searched within
yourself or in others,
try.
It could bring you to new revelations
on your life.
Don't instantly doubt anyone on
something that is not an absolute.
Know that there is little that is
absolutely true,
that you could bet your life on,
without any possible contradiction.
Everyone is a teacher to everyone
else,
whether having a positive or
negative impact.
We all impact another's life
and we should all try to see
everything in a revealing light.

A Question
Christian Hendrix

I wonder if I could hide myself
inside myself
And pop out of this messed up, crazy
world
That has nothing to do with me?

Black and White

Miranda Uphoff

Black and white
The combination is beautiful
You can play them alone.
You can play them together.

Black and white
Both equally glorious in sound
But it's when they're combined
That they grace the world with their
music.

Black and white
God's fingers slide over the keys
Wonderfully combining them
And creating the harmony of the
world.

Coffee Shop

Brianna Hope

The smells hit me the moment I walked through the door. The walls were a dark golden, brushed with a hint of bronze and caramel. The spices and creams were wafting from behind the counter, calling to the customers just arriving inside from the biting cold. Snow was falling out side, and the vivid image of dusk was covering the towering Alpine Mountains, and shadows of blue and violet lurked in the crevices of rock peeking through the snow. I cup my cappuccino in my hands, letting the warmth seep through the cardboard into my skin. I survey the dimly lit room and find a vacant leather chair. I slide over and sit down, leaning back and taking off my coat. I looked up and saw a group of people discussing a book. I looked to my left and saw a couple at a nearby table. They sipped their coffee and stared at each other, while they played a game of Scrabble. I began to wonder about the people who I saw. To distract myself from further thought, I squared my focus on a family to the far right of me. The two parents had three children, all clamoring to have one of the gigantic cookies on display in the glass window near the counter. The mother looked tired but happy, while the father tried to feign impatience with his offspring, though his own sweet tooth showed on his face. I reached for my cup and took a sip. The coffee was soothing to my throat and chest, and as my lips left the cup I noticed a small table, in the far corner of the room. A girl, slightly younger than I was there, sipping on a cup of coffee, just simply staring out the window. She had a view from a small window next to her, and her face was just captivated by the mountains. I could see her features more clearly now, and she was beautiful. Her eyes were a deep violet, and her hair a waving auburn. Her face was oval and thin, with signs of pain and sorrow etched in. I could tell she had a nice smile, although it was clear it hadn't been used in a while. I thought of all the possibilities of her life, how she came to live here, what made her smile. I sipped on my cappuccino for a while, and retracted myself from my surroundings. Deep thought consumed me for a good while, until I realized that I was alone. Except for the girl. She was still there, consumed in her own thought. I finished my drink and threw away the cup, then putting on my coat, I took one last look at the girl, and then walked out into the elements of cold and damp. Taking one last look at the girl through the window, I saw, whilst she was deep in thought, a smile, creep over her face. I in turn smiled, and quickly walked to my car, to head home, to drift into warmth, and to rest for another hectic day, with the coffee shop there to comfort.

Heaven

Brianna Hope

I am just there, a part of the scenery, though probably not as beautiful. The sun warms my heart and body and hits the trees perfectly. The water is crystal clear, and I can see the smooth pebbles and sheets of rock below my feet. The waterfall cascades down in front of me, a picture of paradise. I sink back, and the water reaches my neck. It is cold, and this pleases me. There is something imperfect about this, proving it is real. I lean all the way back and begin to float. I look up at the sky, clear, and cloudless, and dream of the world itself this beautiful. I upright myself, only to find that I don't have the heart to leave. I dive into the water, void of time, with no sense of up or down. My lungs feel like bursting, but I don't care. This is my time, and my body will not interfere. I lose all sense of mind, taking in all sights and sounds. I release air and feel weightless. I propel myself forward and close my eyes. I long for breath, but at the same time fear that if I stop for a moment, I will never get this feeling back. I hear a loud rushing, the rushing of millions of gallons of pain and distraught, worry and spite, fading away. I open my eyes, and find myself directly under the waterfall, the cold numbing my entire body. I ascend next to the water, and feel cold spray hit me with gale and angst. I breathe deeply, the warm air passing through my lungs. Back underneath the water, I feel at home, at peace, and happy, for the first time in a while. I glide easily, slicing through the cold, no longer affected by it. I am able to shape myself into the most calming positions with ease. Letting out some air, I sink to the bottom. The wet sand is warm and smooth. Once again am I pressed to breathe. I shut my eyes in frustration, and rise to the surface angrily, forcing my self not to cry at my limits. Quickly, I immerse myself again, releasing my frustration by propelling myself roughly forward. I close my eyes, happy with my self. I keep moving, toward the sound of the falls. My feet brush a nearby plant, and I don't react, but I am soon intertwined with its slimy fingers, gripping at me forcefully. I become stuck, and my breath has waned. I relax and come free, rising to the top. It has darkened, and the crickets are immersed in their own private choir. I have to be home, back to the stress and worry. I linger a moment, then swim to the shore. I rise, and put on my clothes, shivering at the sudden cold in the air. I walk to my car and turn the key into the lock. I look back one last time, longing to return. I back out of the grass and ramble down the empty backroads of the fontanas. I rest my hands on the wheel and sigh. I have finally found the most wonderful place to get away and relax. I have found Heaven.

Hannah Nodell

Dancers Aren't Normal People
Hannah Nodell

The sound of the feet on the floor
fills my ears.
The sound of my hard work.
I am a dancer.
Day in and day out
different personalities in my dance
company work
to accomplish
the same goal,
to be a great performer.

Normal people just don't understand.
There is this wonderful feeling when
you step out onto that stage.
Everything bad disappears.
It is just you and the dance.
Dancing is the greatest way to
express yourself in the world.

Whatever emotion you are feeling at
that moment,
you can show it through dancing.
If you want to show someone that
you love them,
no matter what kind of love,
you can show them from dancing.
If you are feeling sad and depressed,
you can just let it all out in
movement.
There are so many different ways to
dance,
each way expressing a different
thought or feeling.

The choreographers,
they all come to us wanting us to
experience
something different than ever before.
We all try to understand what they
want to see,
but it is so hard if you cannot see it
yourself.
They continue to work with us until
we get it just right.
" NO, NO, NO," they shout,
"that's not what I want."
I think to myself, " I'm sorry but I
just can't get it."
I may think this, but there is no way
that I will ever show

that I am getting frustrated.
The choreographer comes over to
me,
helps me along with my problems,
finally I can do it right.

We all sit together backstage
before the performance warming our
bodies up.
We do countless swings, stretches,
and contractions
making sure that we dance without
wobbling or messing up.
We don't talk to each other,
But, instead, we think about our
dances and our performance quality.
Right before the curtain opens
we stand in a circle with our hands
held together.
We say our pledge.
" I am an honorable person.
I have a special place in the
ensemble
I promise to perform every dance
with all my energy,
all my power,
with excitement and pride.
I will not fail my dance,
I will not fail my audience,
and I will not fail myself."

We give a final squeeze on each
others hands,
the curtain opens, and the
performance begins.

The music starts
I step onto the stage.
The lights come on.
I feel like I've come to life.
The energy is just bursting out from
me
I give it my all
I hope that the people can see how
much effort I am putting out.
I try my best to show the feeling and
moods
that each dance is supposed to have.
I pray that I don't look silly.
The lights dim
the curtains close,
the performance is over.
The crowd cheers wildly.
" Bravo, Bravo !!"
We take our final bow
and walk backstage.
The sound of feet on the floor fills my
ears,
I am a dancer
This is the sound of my life.
Performing

Searching

Nikki Winters

What's to find in smoky dreams of
the past?
Isn't it describing a future?
A black canvas of dark shadows is in
front of me,
I hold my head…in the confusion.

I'm tired of standing here and being
confused,
Not knowing where to start!
I have to keep running on the right
path,
Not wandering back into the
shadows!
No matter what!
I have to try.

Only I can search for MY future,
Demanding the beat from my heart,
my soul jolts.
Run for your lives dark shadows!
Now slip away back into your
corner!
Forever!

You and Me

Julia Neely

Two people lay beside a tree.
One's name is You and the other's
Me.
You liked to read poetry.
Me liked to write poetry.
Little You looked to Me and said, "I
think I'll write poetry."
Little Me said to You, "I think I'll
change my ways too."
So, little You and little Me,
the two who lay beside the tree,
Decided to change the ways of You
and Me.
Now, You liked to write poetry
And Me liked to read poetry.
Now, reader, can you tell me who
wrote and who read poetry?

Either You or either Me
The two who lay beside a tree.

Twilight Zone

Mackenzie Gill
Kelley Kidd
David Rosseel

Brandy

Kelley Kidd

It was said that every Midwinter's Eve, a strange, beckoning figure would appear on the road to the cemetery. There were many different beliefs about this figure. Some believed that she was as beautiful as an angel: tall and slim with long flowing hair and a golden aura around her. Her gentle, kind, beautiful smile beckoned everyone who saw her to follow. Others believed that she was an old, bent, ugly crone, but when she turned toward you there was sadness in her eyes that forced you to follow out of pity. Some thought the figure was just a darting shadow or a rustle in the bushes that would spark anyone's curiosity. Finally, a few believed anyone present would just hear laughter or crying or some noise in the distance, and they would try to find the source. I, of course, believed none of this. I was not superstitious at all. That was before I met Brandy.

I was a 16 year-old junior in high school, and I had a girlfriend named Desirae. Desirae was amazing; she had forest green, almond shaped eyes, a gorgeous smile, and sand colored wavy hair that fell halfway down her back. She was sweet and had a good sense of humor, but when she had a purpose she was incredibly driven. She held strong in all her beliefs, and she wasn't influenced by anything other people wanted from her; she was just herself, and if you had a problem with that, too bad. Everyone always said that the two of us were a great couple. I use to agree.

It was Midwinter's Eve eve, and, at school, the legend had become the main topic of conversation. I was in a really bad mood, because everyone was teasing me about being non-superstitious.

And, to top it off, Desirae and I got into a fight. It was lunch, and the two of us wandered off to our little table in the back of the cafeteria to eat. We ate in a wonderful silence for the first 10 minutes, but then Desirae had to mess it up.

"You've been really quiet today."

"So what?" I retorted grumpily.

"I was just wondering if you were OK..." she looked hurt, but I didn't care. What right did she have to nose into my life? She was part of my personal life, but not all of it.

"I'm fine, OK? What's your problem?"

"What? Isn't a girl allowed to worry about her boyfriend?"

"Sure, she is, but not when there's nothing wrong!"

"But something is wrong! I'm not stupid, you know!"

"Look, even if something was wrong, which there *isn't*, it wouldn't be any of your business!"

"Yes, it would! I care about you! Is that illegal?"

I hate it when I can't come up with an immediate response, and I was starting to run out of comebacks, so I resorted to saying, "Just leave me alone!"

A single tear began to roll down her cheek, and I turned away. I knew I couldn't look at her face, knew that seeing her cry was too much for me. It wasn't until I had heard her get up out of her chair and walk away that I could turn back around. But, when I tried to finish eating, all traces of my appetite were gone.

The next day had everyone even more excited about the legend, even though I hadn't thought that possible. I don't think anyone talked about anything else the entire day, which meant I didn't talk the whole day, but I had other reasons on top of that. I did, however, see Desirae walking hand-in-hand with a senior I had never seen in my life (probably a football player), and, at lunch, I saw the two eating together. His arm was over her shoulder, and she was leaning into him. I acted like I didn't care, but, inside, I felt like jumping off a cliff.

That day I ate with my best friend, Ryan. Ryan acted kinda

weird, but only because he was shy. His hair was a coppery red and very short, and his bangs hung unevenly into his face. Hidden behind the dark sunglasses that he always wore (even at night) were brown-green eyes. Freckles dotted his long, straight nose, and more dappled his pale cheeks. Purple and blue braces lined his top and bottom teeth, because they had been incredibly uneven since he was seven. I don't remember what we were talking about, but somehow we got on to the subject of Desirae,

"What happened between you two yesterday, by the way?" he asked casually.

"Just a little fight, not anything important," I replied, trying not to think about it.

"If it was 'nothing' than why is she over there with the football captain?"

"Probably trying to make me jealous so I'll switch to her side. Can we drop this?"

"Yeah, sure. I was just wondering. I mean, looking at her now, you would never be able to tell that you even exist."

That was too much. Thinking about her not thinking about me, I couldn't handle it. I stood up and walked away; I didn't even look back at Ryan.

That night, around eight, I went for a walk. I had a little path that I liked to walk on whenever I needed to be alone and think. It happened to go past the cemetery. As I was passing by, curiosity got the better of me, and I wandered off my trail onto the smaller path to the cemetery. I was wandering up the little dirt path slowly, and I glimpsed a figure ahead of me. Squinting through the shadows of the dusk, I managed to make out the silhouette of a figure bending over at a gravestone. The shadow stood up slowly, and, as soon as it stood all the way up, it was gone. Completely petrified and breathing in gasps, I ran back home as soon as I could move again.

Once I was home in bed, I tried to think of some logical version of what had just happened. Banishing all thoughts of the supernatural from my mind, I blamed the low light. Maybe the figure had just stood up and darted away extremely quickly. Maybe I had blinked as soon as the figure stood up, and, by the time I opened his eyes, it had gone too far to see in the dark. Despite all the logical explanations I could think of to explain the incident, the figure in the legend still lingered in the back of my mind, and the thought in my head as I fell asleep was, "What if it is true?"

The next day (Midwinter's Day) the incident from the night before was all I could think about. If anyone found out that I had even considered the legend being true, I would never hear the end of it. That was what I was thinking in biology when she walked in. No one else seemed to notice her, not even our teacher, but she was the most amazing girl I had ever seen. Without drawing any attention to herself, she almost glided across the room and sat right beside me. Mr. Braxton seemed to completely ignore her, and he continued with the lesson.

Throughout the class, I couldn't stop looking at Brandy.

Long locks of auburn hair spilled down over her shoulders, grazing her paper. Everything about her seemed to be graceful and elegant, even the way her pencil moved across her paper. Her nose was a perfect slope, and below it her ruby lips were unreadable. In her deep, black eyes, however, there was a hint of despair. As I watched her, she turned her head and looked directly into my eyes, and I couldn't look away. I felt like I had been turned inside out, and she could see everything in me. I was consumed by her beauty, by the power in her eyes. I heard a voice calling me, but I was too far out of reach. I longed more than anything to just keep staring into her eyes, forever. Why shouldn't I? This was as close to paradise as I would ever be. Why leave? I would just stare into her eyes forever, never go back… And then it was over. She looked away, and I was flung back into the real world with an awful jolt.

"What? Huh?" I looked blankly around the room.

"Oh, good! You've decided to rejoin us here in boring old reality, have you?" Mr. Braxton exclaimed sarcastically. "I was going to have you answer the question on the board, but you seemed otherwise occupied, so I thought I would let you be." Everyone snickered, and I blushed (I always blush; I can't stand it. It seems so girly.). Mr. Braxton gave me a little "should have been paying attention" smile and continued the lesson. Brandy didn't look at me again, thankfully.

That weekend was torture. All I could think of was Brandy: the worlds and worlds I had had traveled through in her eyes, the clear chiming of her laugh, the carefully disguised despair deep in the sea of her eyes, everything… I lived her, breathed her, nothing else was important. I don't think I ate that weekend, just sat in my room thinking of her. I had never been this desperate for a Monday in my life, and I never thought I would want one to come. In the midst of this torture, however, I managed to be rational enough to realize that I had to talk to her, otherwise she might never know who I was. Monday, I decided. I would talk to her when I saw her on Monday.

Without that thought to reassure me, I doubt I would have made it through the weekend.

When I finally returned to school (those are the last words I ever thought I'd say), I realized that I didn't have a single class with her before lunch. Brandy would have to wait until lunch, and in the meantime I had to think about studies. After suffering through three classes, I finally got to see her. She was even more beautiful than I remember. Staring at her, I became completely entranced again. My eyes followed every movement, every toss of her shining hair, every step she took. If I could just get to her… I began to run across the cafeteria to her, but before I could get there, Desirae got in my way. She threw her arms around me and kissed me.

"I'm so sorry. I wish we hadn't fought. I've been tearing myself up about it. Please, please forgive me. Say you're sorry too. Tell me it's OK, please…" My attention strayed to Brandy while Desirae ranted, saying my name over and over.

"Look," I muttered, "I don't have time for this right now, OK? I'll see you around." Pulling myself out her arms, I walked over to Brandy. Since I had to push through everybody to get to her, I didn't reach Brandy until she had sat down. "Seattakenisthis?" Why did I have to screw up right then? In all my daydreams I had imagined me walking up and asking her if I could sit, and then she would swoon and blush and we would talk and fall in love… Now who knew what she thought of me? I tried again, this time emphasizing each word to myself so I didn't lose all my chances, "Is this seat taken?" She smiled that enchanting smile and shook her head. I could feel my stomach doing cartwheels, but I sat, afraid that if I didn't I would do something stupid. I told her my name and stretched out my hand, but she just smiled again.

"I know who you are." Not sure if that was good or bad, I tried to steer the conversation elsewhere.

"How long have you been in town?" That couldn't go too wrong.

"I arrived Midwinter's Eve."

"Have you heard the legend about Midwinter's Eve?"

"Hasn't everyone? Do you guys actually believe in that stuff?"

"I don't. Everyone else does, but I think it's dumb." I sounded like I was trying to suck up to her. "In fact that girl I was with earlier, she was my girlfriend, and… well she's not anymore, that's why we broke up… the legend got us into a big fight…" I trailed off. What was I thinking, telling her all this? I tried to change the subject again; why did I keep screwing this up? "Anyway, where are you from?" After hesitating for a moment, she changed the subject,

"What is there to do here?" she looked right into my eyes when she spoke and immediately forgot the question I had just asked her.

"Lots of stuff. If you want I could take you around to see it all if you wanted…" I still don't know where that line came from. It just rolled out. I could never have come up with that on my own, much less get it out without even stuttering. But it worked wonderfully; she nodded and flashed me that enchanting smile,

"I'd love to. What time?"

"Cool! I'll pick you up Saturday at five, and we can see a movie. If you want we could go to dinner, too."

"I can't wait." A small smile appeared and when I looked into her amazing, deep blue eyes I thought I saw an image of a figure bending down... but she blinked and it was gone. I'm sure it was just me worrying about the legend. Nothing that abnormal could ever appear in such a beautiful thing...

Lunch went well, and conversation between us flowed fairly easily. Everything she said drew me to her more and more. Not only was she the most beautiful girl I had ever seen, she was smart and funny, but still oddly mysterious. Whenever I even thought about bringing the conversation to her past, she would change the subject completely, and I wouldn't even say anything about it. It was almost as though she knew exactly what I was thinking all the time. Sometimes she would even say something half a second before me, and it would be exactly what I was thinking. As soon as she did that, however, she would give me that flirty smile, and everything else would completely leave my mind. Her hand was resting on the table… it would be so easy to just reach across and take it, but what if it scared her? I took a deep breath, and moved my hand toward hers, but, just then, something told me to turn around, and the first thing I saw was Desirae, sitting with her group of friends and crying. Instead of reaching for her hand, I grabbed my drink and took a huge drink out of it.

Walking to class later, I found I couldn't think of Brandy. Desirae was what filled my mind this time. I really needed to get over her. Obviously I didn't like her anymore; I mean, I had Brandy! What did I need Desirae for? She was the one who had gone off with the football captain after our fight. Did she expect me to take her back after what she did to me? She hurt me! But I didn't need her anymore. She probably only came back because her football player dumped her or something.

One Year Later: Midwinter's Day

Something was odd that morning. I could tell the moment I woke up. It felt as though I had woken up from an entire year of dreaming. Glancing at my desk, I saw the earrings and necklace I had bought for Brandy, and instead of the excitement I always felt when I thought of her, I felt a sinking in my stomach. When I tried to picture her perfect face, all I could see was a dark figure bending over a grave in the snow. What was wrong with me? Suddenly, for the first time in almost a year, Desirae came into my mind. Just imagining her face made me burst into tears. I thought I was going crazy. Talking to Brandy would help. It always did. I picked up my phone and dialed her cell phone number. It rang twice before anyone picked up, and when they did, it wasn't her voice answering.

"Hello?"

"Um… Hi. I'm a friend of Brandy's. Is she there…?"

"I'm sorry, who?"

"Brandy Winter's?"

"How do you know that name? Is this some kind of prank?"

"Um… no. I'm her boyfriend. I was wondering if she could go anywhere today,"

"Young man, this isn't funny. The last thing I need is a reminder of my Brandy. Please don't call here ever again." She hung up. I was completely lost. A reminder? Wait… what if she… no, it couldn't be… I ran to the place where I had seen the figure the very first time. Which grave had it been? I thought back to that night, trying to remember where it had been. It was right near the path. I walked beside the graves, trying to remember, and all of a sudden I glanced at one gravestone and saw it.

Brandy Winters. Midwinter's Day, 1980--Midwinter's Day, 1996.

I fell into the snow, praying that this was all a dream. But deep inside me, I knew it wasn't. An icy chill ran through me, and suddenly everything made sense. This was why Ryan never noticed Brandy.

Why no one else had noticed when she walked into Biology that day. Why people gave me weird looks when I went out with her, almost as though they couldn't see her. Why the woman on the phone had sounded so upset. Desirae and I were the only ones that ever knew Brandy was there. If she was.

Desirae. What had I done to her? I had hurt her so much over something that wasn't even there. A ghost. Why me? Why was I the only one that could see her? Or could Desirae see her too? Something crunched in the snow behind me, and I jumped to see who it was. The woman standing there looked exactly like Brandy, except much older. Her skin was wrinkled and her hair had thick streaks of gray growing into it. But she had the same eyes. Those changing, enchanting eyes… and she seemed to recognize me too. She looked almost scared when she spoke, saying my name.

"How do you know my name?!" I was getting a little scared.

"It can't be you… You left right after she died. And you're much too young…"

"I'm sorry, but what are you talking about?"

"I'm sorry young man. I must be scaring you. I'm here to visit my daughter's grave. She died when she was sixteen, and she had a friend that looked just like you. What did you say your name was?" Over her shoulder, she had a black scarf, and she wore an all black outfit. I relaxed a bit and told her my name. She gasped, "Really? That was his name, too. But he would be almost 10 years older than you now."

"This may sound a little odd, but may I tell you something?" She nodded, and I told everything that had happened in the past year. When I had finished, she was almost in tears.

"Thank you for telling me this. Ever since she died, I've felt that there was something she still needed to do. Thanks to you, I think she may be at peace. Finally. I think she just needed to… relive her last year, to make sure everything was right. Without you, she couldn't have ever done it."

As I left the graveyard, I was still trying to comprehend everything that had happened. Brandy was dead. She had been dead for eight years. The figure I had seen on the path was her. I was the only one who could see her because she had loved someone just like me before she died. Now she could finally rest because she had done whatever it was she needed to do. And now she was gone for good. She was just one chapter of my life, and now that she was gone, I realized that she had meant so much to me because it was meant to be. Desirae came to my mind again. How had she known about Brandy? She couldn't see her, could she? I realized then, that it was because we were like one. She knew me so well, she could tell so perfectly what was happening in my mind, she had known something was wrong. She may not have known exactly what it was, but somehow she had realized that something was happening. She knew there was something like Brandy. Because she knew me…

When I thought that, I realized that she was the one I really cared about. I had loved her as long as I had known her, because of who she was, not because she had the power to make me. I knew, right then, that I had to get her back. I had to try to get her to forgive me. She might think I was just desperate, but I had to make her see… I loved her.

Taking a deep breath, I knocked quietly on Desirae's door. The change in her little house was incredible. Remembering how carefully she had groomed her garden, I was stunned when I saw how many weeds had crept into the flowers. The ivy and vines were starting to creep in, and all her flowers looked awful, but what hurt the most were the roses.

At prom I had given her a rose cutting, saying, "Let this grow forever in your garden. Every time it blooms, it'll remind you how much I love you. And when we're apart, look at it so you don't forget." She had looked right into my eyes and said, "I'll never forget."

Ever since then the rose had always been perfectly groomed and watered; it even held the best place in her garden, but now it was wilted and drooping. It even looked as though some of the heads had been ripped or cut off. As I stared out into the jumble of her garden, the door clicked open behind me. Whirling around, I saw that she had changed much more than her garden. In place of her designer clothes was a gigantic T-shirt which hung almost to her knees, and below that I could see the bottom of her baggy shorts. Her perfect, shining hair had become mousy and ratty and was pulled back so clumsily that strands slipped out and hung in her tear-streaked face. The moment Desirae saw me she began to slam the door.

"Desirae, wait! Please!" I called to her through the door. I knew she was standing by the door, wondering what I would say. She would fight with herself for a while, and if I didn't say something to make her open the door now, my chance would be gone. "Desirae, I need to talk to you. I'm an idiot. Brandy… I dunno. It was like I was under a spell. I can't believe I hurt you. I can't believe I kept acting like I did when I knew you were hurt. You shouldn't forgive me. I don't even deserve it, but could you at least give me a second chance? If I screw up this time I'll leave you alone forever. I swear. I brought you something… more roses. Plant them again, start it all over again. It'll be a new beginning, a new relationship, and maybe some of the old one will stay and make us stronger. Desirae? If you're even listening, I want you to know that I love you." It was the first time I'd ever said that to her. I'd implied it, but that was the first time I had said those words. "I do. I love you more than anything. But if you still hate me, I'll understand. I'll leave the roses, plant them to remember me." I left the cuttings by the door and turned to leave, but the door opened, and she stepped out. Tears were streaming down her face. I stepped toward her and held her without a word. After a few minutes, the tears stopped. She looked right into my eyes, just like the night at prom, kissed me, and said,

"I'll never forget. I love you."

David Rosseel

Gorth City

David Roseel

"If you don't have this crate in the truck in ten seconds, I'll blow your brains out you little worm," said a masked figure. "TEN, NINE, EIGHT, SEVEN, SIX, FIVE, FOUR, THREE, TWO, ONE. Time to die, Jackson."

"Ahhhh!" George Jackson woke up from his dream screaming. Doctor Serth came running in.

"What's the matter, Mr. Jackson? I heard you screaming from all the way down the hall," said Serth. Doctor Serth was George's doctor at the Gorth City Mental Institution. George had frequent nightmares that somehow seemed to come true most of the time. Doctor Serth was in the institution to study and mentally evaluate George to see if he was either psychotic, or if his dreams had meaning.

"I had another vision, there was this masked man. He was forcing me to load boxes onto a truck. When I couldn't load the last box on, he shot me," said George.

The year was 1996 and George was a twenty-year-old Harvard undergraduate who was sent to Gorth City, Greenland for mental evaluation. Gorth City was in the most northern part of Greenland, and consisted of around one hundred doctors and two hundred people who worked in the service industry. The city was made up of five apartment buildings for almost all of the people in permanent or temporary residence in the city. There were ten houses that the wealthiest families would live in, a store, which sold everything the city needed, several small businesses, three restaurants, and the Gorth City Mental Institution. The city did not officially exist, and its unofficial existence was not public knowledge. The city no longer stands, due to a horrible 'accident' in 2000.

"Where were you in this dream you had?" asked the doctor.

"It wasn't a dream, it was a vision," exclaimed George angrily.

"I'll be the one to determine that," replied the doctor. "Now, tell me where you were, who the man was, why you couldn't load the last box onto the truck, what was in the b…"

"I don't know!" screamed George. "Besides, if I did know I would have told you a long time ago!"

"You seem to have lost track of reality a very long time ago, Mr. Jackson. If your attitude continues to be this way, we will be forced to move you to an asylum, for you will be beyond help and will need to be isolated from polite society. We cannot risk any negative effect on society due to rash behavior and a lack of sanity."

"I apologize for my behavior, Doctor Serth. It will not happen again," said George.

"Now let's take this slowly from the beginning. What do you

remember from the dream, Mr. Jackson?"

"Well, a masked figure was making me load boxes onto a truck. When I failed to load the last box, he shot and killed me."

"What was in the box, Mr. Jackson?"

"Well, it was labeled 'needles'," George said nervously.

"Possibly a drug operation?"

"Well, there were other boxes labeled 'cotton balls' and 'bandages'."

"So you think they were smuggling medical supplies? Or were they running a drug operation?" inquired the doctor.

"Medical. There were red crosses on some of the boxes."

"So you're positive it wasn't a drug operation?"

"Yes."

"Next question. Where were you?" the doctor demanded.

"Behind a warehouse. It had a sign above the door that said 'Super Safe Warehouse'," said George.

"What city were you in?" asked the doctor.

"The sign said Dallas."

"That's where your parents live, right?"

"Yes, but I've never seen a warehouse called 'Super Safe Warehouse'."

"Is it possible you were just having a strange dream?" asked the doctor.

"I guess so, but it was too vivid, too real to be just a dream," George said nervously. He had no idea what that answer would do to him. It could be what Doctor Serth needed to have him locked away.

"Tell me, George, what do you like to do for fun?" the doctor asked. This was the first time the doctor had addressed George Jackson by his first name.

"Well, I like to watch the football team from my old high school play when visiting home. The Newtonville Zombies, they have an All-American quarter back, Derrick Campbell and a star running ba…"

"Yes, yes, yes," The doctor interrupted. "But do they have sponsors?"

"Yes…" said George nervously.

"What are they?" the doctor asked excitedly.

"Well, there's Super Cheese Pizza, Newtonville Cleaners, the Kitty Kat Grooming Parlor, and some warehouse I can never see the letters for. But there are two words above 'warehouse'."

"There's your dream for you," the doctor said calmly, but in a satisfied tone.

Sometimes you might not notice an advertisement, but when you do it can be stuck in your mind forever. Doctor Serth would normally have written an essay on how this advertisement for 'Super Safe Warehouse' proved his patient was not insane, which might have earned him the Nobel Prize he always dreamed of winning, but he was too busy having arrangements made to have a SWAT team storm the warehouse in order to try to stop the smugglers from operating, and possibly even catch them or discover their identities. This would bring much pride and respect to his family and might save the town or even expand it. This young man, George Jackson, could be what the government needed to declare peace, to start war, or to ensure the well being of all of the people in the world. What George could do and what Doctor Serth could do to help the nation! Of course, there were always alternate routes, routes of greed and of power, routes that would eventually lead to the destruction of Gorth City.

If anyone knew about it, Gorth City would probably be called 'The Sick People City' or 'The Crazy People City', like New York is called 'The Big Apple' or Las Vegas is called 'Sin City.' The secrecy of this isolated town prevented Gorth City from existing, and it's only mentioned when little boys and girls wake up from a nightmare about being shipped off to such a place.

"Mr. Jackson, wake up," the doctor shouted. "I am allowing you to speak with General Jack Holper. He is a very well respected general in The United States Military, and he believes that putting his reputation on the line for your crazy dream is worth his time." Doctor Serth was lying when he said this, of course.

He thought that the dream wasn't crazy, and there was no General Jack Holper. Holper was actually Jack Hopper, and he was a private investigator who frequently figured out cases like this for the mental institution. He would be a huge part in the destruction of the town and would gain from it.

"Hello," George said after answering the phone.

"Hello," the voice on the other end answered. "If you answer all of my questions honestly, your family will not suffer."

"What are you talking about?" George answered nervously.

"Don't be afraid George. I won't kill your mother if you cooperate."

"You can't fool me. You're bluffing, right?" George answered.

"No I'm not," the voice proclaimed angrily.

"I don't believe you. If she's there, put her on the phone."

"If you don't believe me I'll shoot her."

"No! Please don't!" George yelled, breaking out in tears.

"Do you believe me?" the voice demanded.

"No, but I'll still tell you what you want to know," George said. He looked around and noticed that the doctor was gone and the door bolted tight. He was trapped in a situation he should have been able to get out of, but he had a bad hand, and had to throw away the cards. He figured the only way out would be to draw a new hand and choose his cards wisely.

George had been beating around the bush with Jack for five hours, and it was time for him to have dinner. He had been working on making the phone portable all this time and he planned to bolt out the door as soon as it was opened. When the nurse opened the door, he knocked her out from behind and bolted out. He ran through the hallway and out the door, but when he did the alarms sounded.

"You just ran outside, didn't you?" the voice asked.

"Yes, so why don't I hear a gunshot?" George asked.

"I don't have your family hostage," the voice admitted in a

deep, sorrowful tone. "And I don't work for the military. My name is Jack Hopper. I'm a private investigator in this frozen dump of a town. Every night I visit my wife's grave and drink myself to sleep. But enough about me, tell me about your vision."

"I don't have time for this," George snapped. "The security guards are looking for me. If you help me, I'll tell you all about my vision." George was lying, and sadly he wasn't very good at it. He was never a very charismatic person, and it was finally coming back to haunt him.

Jack could tell that George was lying. "No, I don't think it's worth the risk. Besides, I know you're lying George. Most people are a bit better at it than you."

"I don't have to lie all the time like you, Jack. I get through life with honesty and integrity," George said, diving behind a dumpster to avoid detection by a search helicopter sent out by the hospital.

"What was that sound?" Jack asked in a suspicious tone of voice that George could tell wasn't good for his attempt to remain hidden. "Where are you? What are you doing?"

George hung up the phone and buried it in the deep snow. It was only seven degrees out and George was wearing nothing but a hospital gown. He knew he had to get somewhere warm before he died of hypothermia. He considered diving into the dumpster, but the search team would see him, and there were probably dangerous chemicals and used needles from the hospital in it, so he needed to get away some other way. He noticed a guard sitting down in the snow with his back turned away from him and thought that if he could knock out the guard, he could take his gun and clothes. George crawled through the snow and snuck up behind the guard. He grabbed the guard, covered his mouth and smashed a beer bottle he had found behind the dumpster over his head, knocking him out. George dragged the unconscious guard behind the dumpster and repeatedly hit him with his nightstick until he died. George then took the guard's uniform, gun, and nightstick, changed into the uniform, and crept away from the dumpster. When the helicopter flashed its searchlights on him, it just kept searching. George ran down the street and into a near by deli.

"What can me do you for?" the man behind the counter asked. He obviously didn't speak English very well.

"Do you have a car?" George asked.

"Yes, but why did you needs to knows?" the man asked in his strange accent.

"Give me the keys or I kill you!" George screamed at the man, pointing the gun in his face, his hand shaking.

"Yes, I will give you the keyses, jus don'ts shot me. Mine car is the black Toyota."

"I have to shoot you now," George said as the man reached for a gun under the counter. George pulled the trigger, and knew that he had ended a life. He jumped over the counter and grabbed the shotgun from the man and took his keys. He ran out the back door, got into the car, and drove to the power plant.

When George got to the power plant, he grabbed his pistol in his right hand, his nightstick in his left, and slung his shotgun over his back. He planned to beat the guards with his nightstick until they were dead, take their guns, empty the bullets into his pocket, put his nightstick into his belt, and have a gun in two hands. When he did this, he shot down the security cameras and ran into the bathroom. There he took his wooden nightstick and whittled it into a sword. He broke a pipe off to use as a sheath. He ran through the hall and started to shoot random people who posed no threat to him.

George ran to the reactor and blasted down the door with his shotgun. He shot the guards in the room and threw their bodies into the reactor core. This caused the waste to splash all over the room, which weakened the metal on the main reactor tank. He then tossed his wooden sword at the weakened metal and the tank broke. The waste flooded the room and George lit a match and lit a cigarette. He inhaled, exhaled, and dropped the lit cigarette into the waste…

The word of the destruction of Gorth City in 1997 reached the ears of President Clinton very quickly, but there was no record of it until the year 2000. The papers announced that a secret city had been destroyed, but no one cared. They were too concerned with other issues like the Y2K virus.

George Jackson had never had any visions or dreams. He was actually a highly intelligent robot sent to this city to show that greed will be our downfall. The robot could only have survived so long in the snow due to the fact it was a robot, and it was taught to mimic human emotions. You never know when something is a fantasy or reality, and what is good and what is evil, and you never will.

The Memorial Park

Mackenzie Gill

Yes, this is going to be one of those "One day, in a far, far away land...," Except there is one major difference. This far, far away land is in my head. Sometimes I feel there is a far, far away land in my head, and I get lost all alone inside my head. Then again, there are times when I want to be all alone inside my head. Kind of like now.

My mom is making me go to this stupid memorial park where some Civil War battle took place. We are going to have a tour guide who walks us around and reads us some stupid plaque. It will probably be one of those old retired volunteers with one of those orange vests on that makes him look like a crossing-guard. Anyway, so here I am sitting in our old 1987 Volkswagen trying to contain myself from jumping out the door and running home.

We are pulling into the huge parking lot. It has a little ticket box where we have to pay to get in. Who would pay six dollars to get into some old Civil War battle place that probably didn't even exist? "We are supposed to meet our tour guide here," Mom says.

I look out the window. I don't see any tour guide. "Well it seems our tour guide has left without us. Oh well, we have to go home now. Boo Hoo," I say to my mom.

"Nonsense!" she says. "We are just a little bit early that's all."

I sink into my seat and gaze out the window. I think I see a man dressed like he has just stepped off the battlefield. He has a navy-gray suit on with a huge rifle in his hand. I say, "Mom, Mom do you see that man? That man with the big gun in his hand!"

"What man?" Mom asks.

I look out the window and stare across the grassy field where the man had suddenly appeared. I see nothing. I squint my eyes and survey the land. Nothing. The man has disappeared as suddenly as he had appeared. I shrugg my shoulders and listen to the hard rock coming out of my stereo.

We finally find our tour guide and group and after about thirty minutes, I am bored of just hearing about the memorial, so I decide to go to it. I am circling the memorial when I see an old man sitting under the memorial shaped like a dome. He sees me staring at him and beckons me over. I slowly turn away.

Now, I'm not that dim. My mother taught me not to talk to strangers when I was about four. But this old man…he has something different and unique about him. I look at him again. Yes, he seems very nice, sweet, sort of innocent. He is beckoning me over again. My whole brain is saying, "No Roxy, don't do it, it's not right, stop, stop, stop!" But my feet don't agree. My feet walk towards him, and before I know it, I am standing next to him.

He says to me, "What is your name, little girl?"

I don't want to sound like one of those little kids saying, "My mommy told me not to talk to strangers," so I say, "My name is Roxanne, but everybody calls me Roxy."

He asks, "What is your last name, Roxy?"

My last name? Why my last name? What does this guy want? I mean, he's lucky enough that I even came over here, let alone tell him my full name! If my mom even knew I was over here, I would be grounded for a month! Oh well, I decide not to make a big deal about it. "My last name is Anderson." Wow. I'm really contradicting myself today. It's almost like I don't even have a brain!

Just as I say "Anderson" there is a huge blast of blinding white light and the sounds of explosions in the distance. A terrible smell fills the air. It smells of kerosene and rotten eggs mixed together. I open my eyes. I am in the middle of a Civil War fort.

There are about twenty white tents tied down by small ropes and metal stakes. The fort is surrounded by guards carrying big rifles with knives sticking out of the end of their guns. I go up to one of them and_ask, "Where am I?" The man doesn't move a muscle. He completely ignores me. I ask him again, and again, but I don't get a response. He must not be able to hear me. Just in case, I decide to try another guard. I look up at the second guard. There is something vaguely familiar about this guard. But that doesn't seem possible. How could I know a Civil War soldier from almost one hundred and fifty years ago? I think hard. A tiny light bulb goes off in my head. The old man. This soldier is the old man that I had met at the memorial park! But this man must be one hundred and fifty years old! I try talking to the man. I say, "Excuse me sir, what on God's green earth am I doing in a Civil War fort? And on that matter, why on God's green earth are you doing in a Civil War fort?"

The man looks at me and says, "My name is Johnny

Thompson. On this battlefield, I killed a Confederate soldier. That soldier died, and after the battle, I was sitting on that log over there, and I saw the man's soul rise up from the body. It turned out to be a witch, and the witch cursed me so that I would have an immortal life."

So what does that have to do with me? I'm just some random tourist visiting a memorial park. Then he continues talking, "Your family name is the password to go back in time. Anderson. You are the only one who can break the spell. Tonight, the battle will take place again, and I can't kill that soldier, otherwise the witch will come back and curse me forever."

"So all I have to do is say the family name and then I can go back home?"

I look at his face. He is in deep thought. He looks kind of like one of those screwed up mental guys from the soap operas on TV. He stays that way for a while, and then his face lights up. I can tell he has an idea. Sure enough, he does.

"While I am fighting, you have to run to the exact place where the memorial is in mind and say "Anderson." Then you will go back to your time.

Was it really that simple? "How do you know that? How do you know that I won'' be stuck here forever?" I ask him.

He thinks again. "On the wall of the memorial, it told me what to do. It told me to find the girl whose family name is that of the soldier, then redo the battle. It didn't say_anything about the little girl being in the battle. Maybe it was a mistake. Maybe you shouldn't be here." His voice gets more strained and quieter as he speaks.

I shouldn't have been here in the first place, let alone tell some random old man my family name. Anybody knows it is common sense not to talk to an old homeless person. But did I listen to my brain? No. I listened to my heart. "Roxy, if that doesn't work, then I don't think you exist in your world anymore."

Just then, there is a huge blast, a thunder sound deep in the valley. Then the ground starts rumbling like an earthquake. "Run! Run! Go to the memorial place and say Anderson!" he screams. I run. I run the fastest that I've ever run, the wind blowing in my face, bullets whizzing by me and hitting other soldiers. I reach a circle of trees with a big cement platform. I am sure this is the place.

"Anderson!" I yell. Nothing happened. "Anderson! Anderson! Anderson! Anderson!" Nothing happens.

This is the end of me. No more Roxy. Is this really what I deserve? Is this my lesson learned? I learn my lesson, but now, it's too late. Suddenly, I feel cold. I fall to the ground. I look to my side. There is a puddle of blood next to me. I am gone. Gone. No more.

Thirty-four Students
A School's Collection of Stories,
Poems and Thoughts

For information about Greenway School or to order copies of this book, please send correspondence to:

Greenway School
544 Canton Hollow Road
Knoxville, TN 37923
865-777-0197
www.greenwayschool.edu

Printed in the United States
29381LVS00001B/52-111

9 780971 400832